The Critical Idiom

General Editor: JOHN D. JUMP

10 *The Romance*

The Romance/*Gillian Beer*

Methuen & Co Ltd

First published 1970
by Methuen & Co Ltd
11 New Fetter Lane London EC4
© 1970 Gillian Beer
Printed in Great Britain
by Cox & Wyman Ltd, Fakenham, Norfolk

SBN 416 17250 4 Hardback
SBN 416 17260 1 Paperback

Distributed in the U.S.A.
by Barnes & Noble Inc.

Contents

General Editor's Preface

This volume is one of a series of short studies, each dealing with a single key item, or a group of two or three key items, in our critical vocabulary. The purpose of the series differs from that served by the standard glossaries of literary terms. Many terms are adequately defined for the needs of students by the brief entries in these glossaries, and such terms will not be the subjects of studies in the present series. But there are other terms which cannot be made familiar by means of compact definitions. Students need to grow accustomed to them through simple and straightforward but reasonably full discussions of them. The purpose of this series is to provide such discussions.

Some of the terms in question refer to literary movements (e.g. 'Romanticism', 'Aestheticism', etc.), others to literary kinds (e.g. 'Comedy', 'Epic', etc.), and still others to stylistic features (e.g. 'Irony', 'The Conceit', etc.). Because of this diversity of subject-matter, no attempt has been made to impose a uniform pattern upon the studies. But all authors have tried to provide as full illustrative quotation as possible, to make reference whenever appropriate to more than one literature, and to compose their studies in such a way as to guide readers towards the short bibliographies in which they have made suggestions for further reading.

John D. Jump

University of Manchester

Sir, she had read the old romances, and had got into her head the fantastical notion that a woman of spirit should use her lover like a dog. So, Sir, at first she told me that I rode too fast, and she could not keep up with me; and, when I rode a little slower, she passed me, and complained that I lagged behind. I was not to be made the slave of caprice; and I resolved to begin as I meant to end. I therefore pushed on briskly, till I was fairly out of her sight. The road lay between two hedges, so I was sure she could not miss it; and I contrived that she should soon come up with me. When she did, I observed her to be in tears.

(Dr Johnson's account of the journey to church on his wedding morning, recorded by Boswell)

Alice opened the door and found that it led into a small passage, not much larger than a rat-hole: she knelt down and looked along the passage into the loveliest garden you ever saw. How she longed to get out of that dark hall, and wander among those beds of bright flowers and those cool fountains, but she could not even get her head through the doorway; 'and even if my head *would* go through', thought poor Alice, 'it would be of very little use without my shoulders. Oh, how I wish I could shut up like a telescope! I think I could, if only I knew the way to begin.' For, you see, so many out-of-the-way things had happened lately, that Alice had begun to think that very few things indeed were really impossible.

(Lewis Carroll, *Alice in Wonderland*, Chapter 1)

I
History and Definition

Any history of the romance will in one sense be a record of
decadence. The works now popularly called 'romances' are usually
sub-literature, magazines like *True Romances* or lightweight
commercial fiction deliberately written to flatter day dreams.
Such 'romances' batten on the emotionally impoverished. Sub-
literary romances are not new. The circulating libraries provided a
plentiful flow of wish-fulfilment literature in the late eighteenth
and nineteenth centuries and Richard Hoggart, in *The Uses of
Literacy* (London, 1957), demonstrated the functions of such
fiction in a working-class community earlier this century.

It would seem on the face of it that Chaucer had in mind a very
different kind of work when in the sombre opening to *The Book of
the Duchess* he describes himself lying awake, mysteriously griev-
ing, and asks for 'a romaunce' 'to rede, and drive the night away':

> For me thoughte it beter play
> Then play either at ches or tables.
> And in this bok were written fables
> That clerkes had in olde tyme,
> And other poets, put in rime
> To rede, and for to be in minde,
> While men loved the lawe of kinde.
> This bok ne spak but of such thinges,
> Of quenes lives, and of kinges,
> And many other thinges smale.
> Amonge al this I fond a tale
> That me thoughte a wonder thing. (ll 50–61)

This passage characterizes very clearly some of the persisting qualities of the romance and of the relationship between romance and reader.

The tale the poet reads is in verse, re-telling a story written originally in a pre-Christian past when men loved the natural law ('the lawe of kinde'). The figures in the book are aristocratic. He reads for entertainment and for escape from his grief (to 'drive the night away'). 'Amonge al this I fond a tale/That me thoughte a wonder thing': the tale is sorrowful, harmonizing with his own grief and thus allaying it. Chaucer in fact took the 'romance' of Seys and Alcyone from Ovid's *Metamorphoses* (xi, 410 ff) and the version he suggests he is reading is in Guillaume Machaut's *Dit de la Fontaine*.

Romance invokes the past or the socially remote; here it is the pagan world of noble antiquity, a world already separate from that of the 'clerkes' who 'in olde tyme' had put in rhyme its stories – a world even more separate from Chaucer himself who approaches it through a double literary distance of translation and re-interpretation. Ovid was the great source book for courtly love. C. S. Lewis in *The Allegory of Love* points out the paradox that while Ovid's *Ars Amatoria* was pretending to take seriously what his society felt to be a trivial matter (sexual love), the medieval writers took over his examples and treated them with true, almost religious, seriousness. The romance tends to use and re-use well-known stories whose familiarity reassures, and permits a subtly allusive presentation. Its remote sources are domesticated and brought close to present experience primarily because they are peopled with figures whose emotions and relationships are directly registered and described with profuse sensuous detail.

The story Chaucer reads is set in an aristocratic and idealized world entirely peopled with queens and kings (the order in which queen and king appears suggests the influence of courtly love which I shall discuss in the next chapter). But in romance, as in dreams, queens and kings are our representatives. Their royalty universalizes them. They revive our sense of our own omnipotence, which, though constantly assailed by adult experience, survives in the recesses of personality even after childhood.

The story of Seys and Alcyone is a love-story; sexual love is one of the great themes of the romance. It is not, however, quite as universal as is sometimes suggested. In some romances, adventure, which commonly goes alongside love as the great theme and machinery of the work, may take over entirely. The search for treasure, whether it be grail or gold, or dragon's horde, is engrossing enough in itself, and the object of the quest serves as the love-object. *Pilgrim's Progress*, *Treasure Island* and *The Hobbit* are three romance-mutants of this sort.

Chaucer's book spoke of queens and kings 'And many other thinges smale'. There is probably a playful irony in that 'and', but leaving that question aside, it is typical of romance to be much occupied with the everyday paraphernalia of the world it creates. The descriptions of clothes and feasts, the little dogs and the clean towels, give body to its ideal world. They make it physically present. The romance, however lofty its literary and moral qualities, is written primarily to entertain ('me thoughte it beter play/Then play either at ches or tables'). It absorbs the reader into experience which is otherwise unattainable. It frees us from our inhibitions and preoccupations by drawing us entirely into its own world – a world which is never fully equivalent to our own although it must remind us of it if we are to understand it at all. It oversteps the limits by which life is normally bounded. The world of a romance is ample and inclusive, sustained by its own inherent, often obsessive laws. It is not an entire world; it intensifies and exaggerates certain traits in human behaviour and re-creates human figures out of this exaggeration. It excludes some reaches of experience in order to concentrate intently upon certain themes until they take fire and seem to be the flame of life itself.

HISTORICAL DEVELOPMENT

The romance as a literary kind is often exclusively associated with medieval literature. The medieval romances certainly established a pattern which was the dominant form for fiction until perhaps the beginning of the seventeenth century. But the romance has antecedents far back beyond twelfth-century Europe and a vitality which persisted long after the Middle Ages. The Elizabethans call heavily on Greek romances; the 'Western' and science fiction are frequently claimed as modern mutations. In this study I shall explore the resilience of the romance impulse and deliberately emphasize the continuity of its wildly various forms. The term 'romance' in the early Middle Ages meant the new vernacular languages derived from Latin, in contradistinction to the learned language, Latin itself. *Enromancier, romançar, romanz* meant to translate or compose books in the vernacular. The book itself was then called *romanz, roman,* romance, *romanzo.* Then the meaning of the word extended to include the qualities of the literature in these tongues, in contrast to Latin literature or works composed in Latin. Thus, in old French, *romant, roman,* means 'courtly romance in verse', but literally 'popular book'. The characteristics associated with the vernacular literature of the time were a preoccupation with love and adventure and a peculiar vagrancy of imagination. The 'popular' and the 'aristocratic' strains in the romance are already suggested in the term; though the subject-matter of the romances was courtly, its language could be understood by all.

We need to recognize at the start that there is a distinction – but not a constant distinction – between 'the romance' and 'romance' as an element in literature. The history of the romance, like the brief history I have just given of the term 'romance', could almost be epitomized as a shift from form to quality. We tend to speak of 'medieval romances' but of 'the Elizabethan romance' and then of 'romance' in nineteenth-century novels. The word's spectrum of meaning has to be wide to include *Troilus and Criseyde*, *The Faerie Queene*, *The Mysteries of Udolpho* and *Lord Jim*, all of which have been called romances. Keats and Hawthorne both claim the word for one of their works: *Endymion: a poetic romance*; *The House of the Seven Gables: a romance*. Perhaps we can best understand the significance of the romance by considering what kinds of experience it persists in offering the reader through its many guises.

One problem in discussing the romance is the need to limit the way the term is applied. All fiction has a way of looking like romance and in a sense this is just, since all fiction frees us into an imaginative world. But I have limited the description to works which were commonly described by other writers *of the same period* or by the author himself as 'a romance'. I emphasize the first condition because the realistic novels of one age or audience have an uncanny way of becoming 'romances' in another setting. (Richardson's *Pamela* and Trollope's novels are examples.) This is because romance depends considerably upon a certain set *distance* in the relationship between its audience and its subject-matter: the legalistic intricacies of courtly love are discussed in a language open to all; criminal romances of the 'Newgate' type were much read by the law-abiding; novels of high life delight a middle-class audience. The past and the remote distance us all without class discriminations. In some of the finest romances, such as those of Chrétien de Troyes, the ideal world shown is excruciatingly close to the forms of his own society but its imaginative perfection can never be attained in life. To later readers those social forms themselves seem exotic and remote.

The romance is a European form and it is impossible to understand its significance in English literature without recognizing that many of the greatest romance writers wrote in other tongues and earlier than our authors. Chrétien and Ariosto are two major examples. There is an element of *enromancier*, of translation into the vernacular, in the achievement of Malory and even Spenser. Although I have claimed that the romance is a European form, from the time of the crusades its achievement has been affected by the culture of the East, and from the eighteenth century down to E. W. Lane's scholarly and sociological translation (London, 1839–41), particularly by *The Arabian Nights*.

The romance was an important genre in English literature in the fourteenth and fifteenth centuries; in the Elizabethan period; in the eighteenth century, with its gradual polarization of the romance and the novel. The Gothic romance and the romantic movement gave new significances to the form, and in the nineteenth century the romance was developed as a challenge to the deterministic French novel as well as being revived intact by the Pre-Raphaelites. I shall discuss each of these periods in some detail in the sections following the introduction.

Two major types of the romance, which for convenience we may call the aristocratic and the popular, have come down to us, sometimes converging, sometimes standing in opposition. They call on the same themes and properties but differ in scale. The aristocratic romance, such as that of Malory or Ariosto, makes clear its descent from the epic; it is a large-scale work interweaving many narrative threads. The popular romance tends towards simplicity and concentration, as in the ballad. It sets out to tell a single story. We could take *Le Grand Cyrus* and *Havelok the Dane* as typifying the two traditions, but it is not very profitable to attempt any absolute polarization. The two kinds have too much in common and in the light of history their distinctions blur.

There are two major turning-points in the history of the romance in England; they both have to do with an increasing self-consciousness about the way the form is used. The first was the publication of Shelton's translation of *Don Quixote* in 1612 and 1620. (Cervantes had published the work in two parts in 1605 and 1615.) The second was the 'romantic revival', bringing with it the conscious antiquarianism with which writers of the Romantic period viewed the romance. In both cases the effect was to mark out the province of the romance as the remote and the impossible and to introduce an inhibiting consciousness. But whereas the immediately post-Cervantic attitude to romance tended to establish the exclusiveness of the romance world, thus increasing the danger of frivolity, writers of the Romantic period, such as Schlegel and Coleridge, recognized that the romance expressed a world permanently within all men: the world of the imagination and of dream.

Until after Spenser the romance was still very much the dominant form of fiction and it was quite as often written in verse as in prose. With the gradual rise of the novel, however, it tended to be in prose and to be *in reaction*. The later history of the romance is inextricable from the development of the novel. Clara Reeve, in her excellent history, *The Progress of Romance* (London, 1785), assumed that the romance was being replaced by the novel. She claimed that the romance went back as far as the ancient Egyptians and she urged its antiquity as evidence of its literary respectability. 'Epic poetry is the parent of romance' she asserted as part of her spirited defence of a form which was at the time suspect on both moral and intellectual grounds. Her own novel *The Old English Baron: A Gothic Tale* was among the early Gothic romances whose use of mystery, antiquarianism and emotional extremes challenged the restraints of rationalism. And that, whether deliberately or not, has been one persisting function of the romance.

In our own century the work of Freud and Jung, while making many artists and critics distrustful of self-indulgent fantasy, has also made them far more aware of the force of the subconscious. This has liberated elements of experience earlier associated with the romance and allowed the modern novel to thrive on allegory and dream, to invoke what is mythic within our own world. Patrick White's *Voss*, Hermann Hesse's *Steppenwolf*, Maurice Jouffroy's

Un Rêve plus Longue que la Nuit, Saul Bellow's *Henderson the Rain King*, perhaps even Günther Grass's *The Tin Drum* – these disparate novels show how richly the 'romance' tradition is still yielding in recent literature. But nobody, I think, would call them 'romances': the term itself has an old-fashioned ring.

THE ROMANCE AND THE READER

Although some of the literary properties of romance have changed beyond recognition over the centuries, many of its imaginative functions remain constant. The relief the romance offered to the poet in *The Book of the Duchess* is not utterly different in kind from that offered by the commercial romances of our own time. This is not to dignify pulp literature or to debase the complex and profound experience offered by the finest romance writers. I want to emphasize, however, the extent to which the romance can be distinguished from other forms of fiction by the relationship it imposes between reader and romance-world. This relationship liberates us but it also involves unusual dependency.

The romance is essentially subjective, although the personality of the writer may be expressed only through the work itself, not as a personal presence. We have to depend entirely on the narrator of the romance: he remakes the rules of what is possible, what impossible. Our enjoyment depends upon our willing surrender to his power. We are transported. The absurdities of romance are felt when we refuse to inhabit the world offered us and disengage ourselves, bringing to bear our own opinions. Malory's *Morte D'Arthure* and Mrs Radcliffe's *The Mysteries of Udolpho* will each appear ridiculous if we refuse to acquiesce in the courtly code or the 'sublime'.

The romance requires of us the wholehearted involvement which a child feels in a story told; in that sense there is something 'child-like' in the pleasure of romance.

He holds him with his glittering eye –
The Wedding-Guest stood still,
And listens like a three years' child:
The Mariner hath his will.

The Ancient Mariner dominates the wedding-guest while he tells his story: the experience is terrible as well as pleasurable. Post-romantic writers have emphasized the authoritarian in the romance situation. Kafka's *The Castle*, for instance, uses many of the traditional elements of romance. The grip of a romance can be that of a dream or of nightmare.

It is our relationship to the narration which has an affinity with a child's experience, not the world portrayed or the insights which compose it. And of course any adult participating in such a relationship is likely to do so with a sense of relief and of sophistication. The romance rarely attempts to dislodge our hold on reality completely. The comfort of being told a story mingles with aesthetic elation. Part of the delight of the romance is that we know we are not required to live full-time in its ideal worlds. It amplifies our experience; it does not press home upon us our immediate everyday concerns.

Yet the finest romances are always much preoccupied with psychic responsibilities. Because romance shows us the ideal it is implicitly instructive as well as escapist. By removing the restraints of rationalism it can reach straight to those levels of our experience which are also re-created in myth and fairy-tale. By simplifying character the romance removes the idiosyncrasies which set other people apart from us; this allows us to act out through stylized figures the radical impulses of human experience. The rhythms of the interwoven stories in the typical romance construction correspond to the way we interpret our own experience as multiple, endlessly interpenetrating stories, rather than simply as a procession of banal happenings.

One quality not so far mentioned is the use of the 'marvellous' and the supernatural. This is sometimes taken to be the hall-mark of romance but it is crucial only in the seventeenth- and eighteenth-century romance, although it has a definite and limited role in the Arthurian cycles and occurs in a muted 'secularized' form in works like Conrad's *The Shadow-Line*. I shall discuss the uses of the supernatural in various periods of the romance in the sections below.

It might legitimately be objected that the qualities I have defined as characterizing the romance are all to be found elsewhere in literature, and particularly in other types of fiction. This is true. There is no single characteristic which distinguishes the romance from other literary kinds nor will every one of the characteristics I have been describing be present in each work that we would want to call a romance. We can think rather of a cluster of proper-ties: the themes of love and adventure, a certain withdrawal from their own societies on the part of both reader and romance hero, profuse sensuous detail, simplified characters (often with a suggestion of allegorical significance), a serene intermingling of the unexpected and the everyday, a complex and prolonged succession of incidents usually without a single climax, a happy ending, amplitude of proportions, a strongly enforced code of conduct to which all the characters must comply.

THE ROMANCE AND THE NOVEL

All fiction contains two primary impulses: the impulse to imitate daily life and the impulse to transcend it. It would be hard to think of any satisfying work of literature which totally excludes either. Let us take two extreme examples. Defoe's fiction never acknow-ledges that it is not fact. It draws much of its energy from objectiv-ism (records of bills, detailed accounts of escape routes through named London streets, the processes of making things, the details of trading). Yet even his books thrive on his characters' fantasies about themselves. Moll Flanders, in her own eyes, is never simply a 'moll', a whore; she feels herself to be a lady and she is determined to live the life of a lady. The book's richness lies in the stresses and strains between Moll's aspirations and her ways and means of survival. Malory's *Morte D'Arthure* is avowedly set in an ideal past known of only through literary sources which leave many of the customs of that time mysterious: 'For, as the Freynshhe booke seyth, the quene and sir Launcelot were togydirs. And whether they were abed other at other maner of disportis, me lyste nat thereof make no mencion, for love that tyme was nat as love ys nowadayes.' ('The Most Piteous Tale of the Morte Arthur Saunz Gwerdon' in *The Works of Sir Thomas Malory*, ed. E. Vinaver (Oxford, 1947) vol. III, p. 1165). But any idea that the romance is vague and remote is dispelled by the scene which immediately follows the quotation above. Sir Mordred and other knights come to the bedchamber where Launcelot and Gwenyver are, and attempt to break in. The characters come close to our known world through the rhythms of their dialogue. We hear human voices speaking, passionate and equivocal in crisis.

'Alas!' seyde quene Gwenyver, 'now ar we myscheved bothe!'

'Madame', seyde sir Launcelot, 'ys there here ony armour within you that myght cover my body wythall? And if there be ony, gyff hit me and I shall sone stynte their malice, by the grace of God!'

'Now, truly,' seyde the quyne, 'I have none armour nother helme, shylde, swerde, nother speare, wherefore I dred me sore oure longe love ys com to a myschyvus ende. For I here by their noyse there be many noble knyghtes, and well I wote they be surely armed, and ayenst them ye may make no resistance. Wherefore ye are lykly to be slayne, and than shall I be brente! [burnt] For and ye myght ascape them,' seyde the quene, 'I wolde nat doute but that ye wolde rescowe me in what daunger that I ever stood in.'

'Alas!' seyde sir Launcelot, 'in all my lyff thus was I never bestad that I shulde be thus shamefully slayne, for lake of myne armour.'

The violent practical need for armour to cover his nakedness obsesses Launcelot, while Gwenyver, with the rapid concentration of disaster, looks beyond the present to her own death at the stake. The love between them is implicit, declared briefly in that one word 'longe' ('I dred me sore oure longe love ys com to a myschyvus ende.'). The human impulses of fear, self-concern, courage and despair are expressively rendered in the sinews of the dialogue.

Defoe's facts and objects are given significance by being related to Moll's inner experience and aspirations. Malory's generalized high-wrought world of the fabled past is made present to us in the passage quoted and in the rest of the scene, through the rhythms of human speech barely stylized and perfectly articulated in a moment of extremity.

Whereas in the earlier part of its history, when it was the dominant form for fiction, the romance can be quite reliably recognized by its subject-matter, the distinction between novel and romance later becomes a matter of the balance of attention. The novel is more preoccupied with representing and interpreting a known world, the romance with making apparent the hidden dreams of that world. Romance is always concerned with the fulfilment of desires – and for that reason it takes many forms: the heroic, the pastoral, the exotic, the mysterious, the dream, childhood, and total passionate love. It is usually acutely fashionable, cast in the exact mould of an age's sensibility. Although it draws on basic human impulses it often registers with extraordinary refinement the peculiar forms and vacillations of a period. As a result it is frequently as ephemeral as fashion and, though completely beguiling to its own time, unreadable to later generations. Clara Reeve's Euphues in *The Progress of Romance* comments on the vast French romances of the seventeenth century:

> These were the books that pleased our grandmothers, whose patience in wading thro' such tremendous volumes, may raise our surprise: for to us they appear dull, – heavy, – and uninteresting.

The romance gives repetitive form to the particular desires of a community, and especially to those desires which cannot find controlled expression within a society. This is another reason why works which read like realistic fiction to the audience to whom they were first addressed, read like romance to future generations.

Pamela is a case in point. Richardson's novel of the maidservant who withstood her master's advances and then married him gave lineaments to many covert desires and expressed the fantasies of a wide social range of readers. Pamela is an ideal figure as well as a lively young woman (she shares her name with one of the perfect heroines of Sidney's romance *Arcadia*). Few maidservants could hope to withstand the assaults of their master and win through to marriage and enfranchisement; few men could hope for erotic and lawful gratification from a wife who was their servant and their moral superior. The book was in a sense revolutionary, undermining the common assumptions about the outcome of such a story. Fielding's suggestion that Pamela was simply a hypocrite was a convenient way of slotting her back into a conservative picture of social roles and personality. But the book's immense popularity came from more than a prurient pleasure in the long siege of Pamela's virtue. It was based also on scarcely formulated longings and ideals which were hampered by the actual social system and by the current assumptions about the relationships between men and women. The closely realistic narrative surface allowed its first audience to accept it as a report from life without bringing to consciousness the ways in which it released them from the inhibitions of their own society. Revolution is one function of the romance. But when the revolutionary situation is past, readers come to interpret the text nostalgically.

OBJECTIONS TO THE ROMANCE

Only the finest works of art can survive the shifting needs of readers and this is peculiarly so in the romance form which sets out to satisfy contemporary appetites. Its value may be quickly consumed. But perhaps its principal *artistic* problem is, quite simply, that it tends to bore the reader who does not succumb totally to it. The principal *moral* objection which has continuously been made to it is that it seduces the reader: it offers him a kind of fairy world which will unfit him (or more frequently her) for common life after he has sojourned there. The two objections are not unconnected. Pamela pronounces upon 'novels and romances' in the last pages of the second volume:

> there were very few novels and romances that my lady would permit me to read; and those I did, gave me no great pleasure; for either they dealt so much in the *marvellous* and *improbable*, or were so unnaturally *inflaming* to the *passions*, and so full of *love* and *intrigue*, that most of them seemed calculated to *fire* the *imagination*, rather than to *inform* the *judgment*. Titles and tournaments, breaking of spears in honour of a mistress, engaging with monsters, rambling in search of adventures, making unnatural difficulties, in order to show the knight-errant's prowess in overcoming them, is all that is required to constitute the *hero* in such pieces. And what principally distinguishes the character of the *heroine* is, when she is taught to consider her father's house as an enchanted castle, and her lover as the hero who is to dissolve the charm, and to set at liberty from one confinement, in order to put her into another, and, too probably, a worse: to instruct her how to climb walls, leap precipices, and do twenty other extravagant things, in order to show the mad strength of a passion she ought to be ashamed of; to make parents and guardians pass for tyrants, the voice of reason to be drowned in that of indiscreet love, which exalts the other sex, and debases her own. And what is the instruction that can be gathered from such pieces, for the conduct of common life?

Pamela here summarizes most of the objections which have been made to the romance since it began to be an outlaw literary form in the seventeenth century: it drowns the voice of reason, it offers a

dangerously misleading guide to everyday life, it rouses false
expectations and stirs up passions best held in check. One objection
she does not use – because it does not concern her – is the lack of
intellectual power which some later writers have held against the
romance.

The romance experience as Pamela describes it is hectic and
robust. A century later in *Madame Bovary* Flaubert suggests that
the romances which help to deprave Emma's sensibility and
nourish her illusions have a fusty decrepitude about them:

> Ce n'étaient qu'amours, amants, amantes, dames persécutées s'évan-
> ouissant dans des pavillons solitaires, postillons qu'on tue à tous les
> relais, chevaux qu'on crève à toutes les pages, forêts sombres, troubles
> du coeur, serments, sanglots, larmes et baisers, nacelles au clair de
> lune, rossignols dans les bosquets, *messieurs* braves comme des lions,
> doux comme des agneaux, vertueux comme on ne l'est pas, toujours
> bien mis, et qui pleurent comme des urnes. Pendant six mois, à
> quinze ans, Emma se graissa donc les mains à cette poussière des
> vieux cabinets de lecture. Avec Walter Scott, plus tard, elle s'éprit
> de choses historiques, rêve à bahuts, salle des gardes et ménestrels.
> (Book I, Chapter 6)

> (They were all about love and lovers, damsels in distress swooning in
> lonely lodges, postillions slaughtered all along the road, horses
> ridden to death on every page, gloomy forests, troubles of the heart,
> vows, sobs, tears, kisses, rowing-boats in the moonlight, nightingales
> in the grove, gentlemen brave as lions and gentle as lambs, too
> virtuous to be true, invariably well-dressed, and weeping like
> fountains. And so for six months of her sixteenth year, Emma soiled
> her hands with this refuse of old lending libraries. Coming later to
> Sir Walter Scott, she conceived a passion for the historical, and
> dreamed about oak chests, guardrooms, minstrels.)
> (Tr. Alan Russell, Penguin Classics, Harmondsworth, 1950, p. 1150)

And in *Ulysses* Joyce apes poor Gertie MacDowell's slack and
self-indulgent consciousness through an apparently uncritical
description of her in the terms of romantic fiction:

There was an innate refinement, a languid queenly *hauteur* about Gerty which was unmistakably evidenced in her delicate hands and higharched instep. Had kind fate but willed her to be born a gentlewoman of high degree in her own right and had she only received the benefit of a good education Gerty MacDowell might easily have held her own beside any lady in the land and have seen herself exquisitely gowned with jewels on her brow and patrician suitors at her feet vying with one another to pay their devoirs to her.

(London, 1937, p. 332)

As these passages show, the chivalric and aristocratic imagery of the romance is extraordinarily constant. Each of them glances at a different kind of romance (French seventeenth century, Gothic historical, and 'silver fork').

The romance constantly tends towards decadence but the impulses which give rise to the form are too powerful for it ever to be completely abandoned. Henry James seized one central attribute of the form, and one reason for its continued fruitfulness, when he wrote in the Preface to *The American* (1877) of its free intensity:

The only *general* attribute of projected romance that I can see . . . is the fact of the kind of experience with which it deals – experience liberated, so to speak; experience disengaged, disembroiled, disencumbered, exempt from the conditions that we usually know to attach to it and, if we wish so to put the matter, drag upon it, and operating in a medium which relieves it, in a particular interest, of the inconvenience of a *related*, a measurable state, a state subject to all our vulgar communities. The greatest intensity may so be arrived at evidently – when the sacrifice of community, of the 'related' sides of situations, has not been too rash.

René Wellek puts it another way in *The Theory of Literature*, (London, 1949): 'the romance is poetic or epic: we should now call it "mythic"' (p. 223). The 'mythic' element in romance is vital to an understanding of the form in the period to which we now turn for a consideration of medieval and renaissance romance.

2

Medieval to Renaissance Romance: History and Myth

Medieval romance as a genre was separate from epic or allegory, though it had elements of both. It allowed a casual interplay between history and miracle. Love and adventure in the romance were both presented through a ritualized code of conduct, but although this code was preoccupied with niceties of behaviour it recognized and accepted irrational impulses and unforeseeable actions. The writers could encompass the marvellous and the everyday without any change of key. The romances often included complex psychological analysis – particularly in the work of writers like Chrétien de Troyes and Hartmann von Aue in his refashioning of Chrétien's romances – yet its insights were not primarily analytical; instead its significance evolved out of the interpenetrating levels of event.

The romance writer's mediating presence allows us to accept what he shows. He will intervene to comment and interpret, controlling the tone in such a way that he seems to bestow upon us a certain grace and dexterity of response and absolve us from the need to make full-scale 'interpretations'. The matter of the romances is open; its system of values is set before us within the poems themselves; its mythic levels of suggestion require no arcane knowledge. The central delight offered us is that of being told a story.

This is not to say that the medieval romances are 'primitive'; they demand alertness and application from the reader. Clearly

there are differing degrees of literary sophistication among medieval romance writers, but the finest of them display a broad and
assured literary consciousness such as we find in Chaucer.

The medieval romance writers suggest the infinity which every-
where touches upon the world they display without resort to the
fully sustained fourfold system of medieval allegory: the literal,
allegorical, tropological and anagogical levels. Allegory is one
strand in the artistry of the romance; only in the Grail romances
is there any thoroughgoing commitment to it, and even there the
shining chalice of the Grail achieves total and defined meaning as
an object. Where allegory is intended, its presence is well-sign-
posted and its interpretation clear cut. In *The Romaunt of the Rose*,
for example, the whole is written from the man's point of view
with the lady as the rose; the characters have names like Faire-
Semblaunt and Strayned-Abstynaunce, and Guillaume de Lorris
who wrote the earlier and simpler section of the poem invites the
reader to:

> so long abide,
> Tyl I this Romance may unhide,
> And undo the signifiance
> Of this drem into Romance. (ll 2167–70)

Even among writers who eschew this emblematic view of allegory
the symbols are usually organically related to normal experience:
the spring, a garden, landscapes fair or wasted, white, black.
There is no difficulty in interpreting such signs – though perhaps
we should not forget that medieval literature crystallized the ability
to read such literature with ease.

> Alone I wente in my plaiyng,
> The smale foules song harknyng,
> That peyned hem, ful many peyre,
> To synge on bowes blosmed feyre.
> Jolif and gay, ful of gladnesse,
> Toward a ryver gan I me dresse,

> That I herd renne faste by;
> For fairer plaiyng non saugh I
> Than playen me by that ryver.
> For from an hill that stood ther ner,
> Cam doun the strem ful stif and bold.
>
> (*Romaunt of the Rose*, ll 105–15. The translation is Chaucer's)

At the same time – as this passage suggests – the romance writers draw upon archetypal patterns which meet an understanding in the reader without necessarily formalizing into consciousness. In this aspect the romance is akin to fairy-tale and preserves some of the mystery of its Breton origins. Several modern commentators, notably Northrop Frye and Friedrich Heer, have emphasized the Jungian force of the romance. In *The Anatomy of Criticism* (Princeton, 1957) Frye devotes one section of his brilliant theoretical work on Archetypal Criticism to 'The Mythos of Summer: Romance', but it is in the Fourth Essay on the 'Theory of Genres' that he analyses the narrative methods of romance and brings out what is peculiar in romance-characterization:

> The romancer does not attempt to create 'real people' so much as stylized figures which expand into psychological archetypes. It is in the romance that we find Jung's libido, anima, and shadow reflected in the hero, heroine, and villain respectively. That is why the romance so often radiates a glow of subjective intensity that the novel lacks, and why a suggestion of allegory is constantly creeping in around its fringes. (p. 196)

Heer, speaking more specifically of medieval romance, emphasizes some of the same characteristics through a discussion of recurring plot-patterns:

> The *roman courtois* did not ignore the energizing springs of life, the deeper layers of personality: they encompass life as a whole ... The skill in 'depth psychology' found in these romances is astonishing (at least to anyone ignorant of the wisdom that myths and fairy-tales

habitually display in these matters). Embedded in them are all the father and mother motifs, used to illuminate the relations of the hero with his parents; and more than this, they often confront us with two sets of pairs in opposition to each other in a quaternity which brings to mind the researches of Jung.

(Friedrich Heer, *The Medieval World*, tr. J. Sondheimer, London, 1962, p. 144)

We cannot, of course, reverse this argument and claim as romances all works of fiction which use such quaternity, or we would find ourselves including, for example, Lawrence's *Women in Love*. In the same way, the dream form is not peculiar to romance (though it might be claimed that it is learnt from romance by writers such as Langland and Bunyan). But it is continuously used by writers of romance from Chaucer to Keats, and its unstable blending of the actual and the symbolic is typical of the romance method, which constantly allows appearance and significance equal presence.

What distinguishes the medieval romances is the way in which they make available and apparent simultaneously all their preoccupations. Nothing is subordinated. C. S. Lewis suggested the phrase 'polyphonic narrative' for the organization of such works. In music, polyphony is a form in which the various voices move in apparent independence and freedom though fitting together harmonically. This is an apt metaphor for romance narration where very varied characters and episodes move freely while at the same time being interwoven to compose a congruent whole. The action is intricate, often dense, but the polyphonic form means that the intensity is based on the senses (bright colours, sounds, swift changes of scene, beautiful women, elaborate descriptions of architecture and ornament). It is rarely an intensity of plot-climax. The crucial or violent episodes tend to be recorded in the same narrative tone as the descriptions. If we are to understand the romance method we have to abandon the critical metaphors of perspective (with its suggestion of far and near) or depth (with its suggestion that what is deepest is most significant). Instead we are presented with a thronging, level world, held at a constant distance from us, colourful, full of detail and particularity, ramifying endlessly outwards. The characteristic narrative device is that of 'entrelacement', interlacing stories so that nothing is ever finally abandoned or circumscribed. Vinaver compares the effect to that of medieval ornament:

> The expansion is not, as in classical ornament, a movement towards or away from a real or imaginary centre – since there is no centre – but towards *potential infinity*.
>
> (*Form and Meaning in Medieval Romance*, 1966)

Some of the characteristics of medieval romance are those commonly found in oral literature, and we know that many romances were never written down and so have perished. They were recited to musical accompaniment before an audience, perhaps the assembled court or a feudal household and the reciter could display his skill as an actor by impersonating a great range of characters: ladies and giants, knights and sage commentators. This may in part account for the popularity of debate in many of the works. It is almost certainly one of the reasons for the infinite extension allowed by 'entrelacement' and for the immersion in the present which is characteristic of the romances. The romances which survive are those which were also written down. Some are the result of accretion but many bear the stamp of a single mind even when the material has been used elsewhere. And in the case of Chrétien de Troyes we have an extraordinary example of a single writer of genius more or less establishing the literary popularity of a body of material – that of the Arthurian cycle – which is then disseminated throughout Europe and beyond. Chrétien did not invent the world of Arthur, the *Matière de Bretagne*, but he was the first to exploit the vogue of Arthur in long verse romance and to give it a harmonious form.

MEDIEVAL CHIVALRIC ROMANCE

The fame of Arthur was an extraordinary phenomenon in the twelfth century. R. S. Loomis in his *Arthurian Tradition and Chrétien de Troyes* (New York, 1949) quotes Alanus de Insulis's rhapsodic claim that 'he is but little less known to the peoples of Asia than to the Bretons ... Egypt speaks of him and the Bosphorus is not silent.' What concerns us here is the way in which the legends were used by medieval writers of courtly romance and the way in which the Arthurian preoccupation with love created a new imaginative theme, set in tension with the *chanson de geste*'s preoccupation with feats of arms and honour. Medieval tradition early recognized two distinct 'matters' of Arthur – the historical and the fabulous. For example, William of Malmesbury wrote: 'It is of this Arthur that the Britons fondly tell so many fables, even to this present day; a man worthy to be celebrated not by ideal fictions, but by authentic history.' But the demarcation between the two 'matters' was not easy to establish, and the romance thrives in the shifting borderland between legend and fact. The Arthurian cycle offered a combination of history and myth which was particularly acceptable to a society intent upon mythologizing itself. The courts of Eleanor of Aquitaine and her daughter Marie de Champagne, with their elaboration of 'courtly love', formed such a society.

I will not attempt here a full description of the code and practice of courtly love in its relation to literature, since this is set out in detail in C. S. Lewis's *The Allegory of Love*. The courtly love code adopted the terms of law and religion, their quibbles and ecstasies, but shifted the poles of their significance. The vital relationship is not now between man and society, man and God, but between two lovers: the lady and her 'man'. Andreas Capellanus, Marie's court chaplain, summarized the Code of Love in thirty-one Articles in a small treatise, *De Arte Honeste Amandi*, and Eleanor staged a grand assize, a 'court of love', at Poitiers in which the wire-drawn distinctions of the courtly code were argued out by the judging ladies while the men sat as suitors below.

The courtly code was in its way revolutionary. It subverted the values of feudal society by its emphasis on love without bargains, its fantasy of female dominance, its individualism and its paradoxical legalism which piquantly appropriated the language of authority while undermining authoritarian assumptions. It is this coming together of political actuality and imaginative creation which gives special power to writers such as Chrétien. Unlike many later romance writers he is not reviving the *past* wonders of jousts and tournaments, of a world where the passionate niceties of love were practised. He is rather offering an imaginative idealization of the world about him. This world was itself committed to the idealization of courtly life, so that he is able to use the details of actual costumes and feasts and events familiar in twelfth-century France while representing its ideals with an intense perfection which could find form only in literature.

Chrétien, and a little later Hartmann von Aue and Gottfried von Strassburg, were producing psychologically radical, not nostalgic, works of art. Conservatism was always an impulse in the romance: we see it magnificently at work in Wolfram von Eschenbach's *Parzifal* with its reassertion of the power of empire and honour. But revivalism became a habitual part of the romance only when the issues satirized and embodied by courtly love were no longer incendiary. Knights and jousts, arranged marriages, the power of the Court and of the Emperor, were the actuality of these early writers.

Dorothy Everett, and more recently Rosamund Tuve, have emphasized the essential 'realism' of the medieval romances. Miss Everett suggested that they pleased their original audience 'as modern novels of "high life" do'. ('A Characterization of the English Medieval Romances', *Essays and Studies*, XV, 1929.)

Miss Tuve commented: 'To be sure, romances were a genre that portrayed life idealistically, but on the assumption that it was a realistic portrayal of life.' (*Allegorical Imagery*, Princeton, 1966.) In *Mimesis* (Princeton, 1953), Erich Auerbach suggests with absolute precision the balance in the romances: 'The Fairy-tale atmosphere is the true element of the courtly romance, which after all is not only interested in portraying external living conditions in the feudal society of the closing years of the twelfth century but also and especially in expressing its ideals' (p. 127).

In this atmosphere the magical and the political easily became linked. Heer reminds us that Eleanor of Aquitaine had her son installed as Duke of Aquitaine through a symbolic marriage ceremony between Richard and the legendary St Valery, patroness of the region. Many of the *chansons de geste* were commissioned by French feudal families who prided themselves on tracing their descent from chieftains of the fabulous ages of society. For example, rather at the end of the tradition in the fourteenth century the family of Lusignan employed Jean d'Arras to compile the romance of *Melusine*, telling the story of the marriage of one of their great chiefs to a fairy who every Saturday took the form of a serpent. Such late *chansons de geste* are often scarcely distinguishable from romance. By this period romance is an inclusive, not a defining term. But it is possible to distinguish between the two interconnected forms at an earlier period before romance had become dominant.

The old French epic, the *chanson de geste*, finds its noblest form in the *Chanson de Roland*. In England, *The Battle of Maldon* shows some of the same respect for loyalty and prowess but without the individual passions of *Roland*. The *chanson de geste* is essentially active, martial, peopled by men and heroes; the romance tends to be contemplative and to give a major role to women and to affairs of love. True, combat is still the test of the romance hero but the motivation for combat has to some extent changed. Whereas the *chanson de geste* hero fights in a public cause, the romance hero usually fights for a private ideal of behaviour. Moreover, combat is no longer the central crisis, even in a work like *Sir Gawain and the Green Knight* where the fight provides the climax of the action. The increased role of women and the emphasis on sexual love chiefly distinguish the Arthurian romance from earlier related Carolingian literature. This helped to establish the 'feminine' temper of the genre. At its worst, this has turned the romance into indolent and self-regarding entertainment, as in the late seventeenth century. At its best, however, it has given great importance to individualism and to human relatedness, to discrimination and passion.

Moreover, I think we should take to heart Rosamund Tuve's reminder (in *Allegorical Imagery*) that sexual love, in its rarefied expression, courtly love, is by no means the only form of ideal love the romances demonstrate to us:

> we read a great deal about love as that term embraces an endless variety of human affections – the poignancy of the relationship between Gawain and Lancelot, the love Galehaut bore Lancelot, sudden ungovernable desires or *folies*, consistently faithful devotion, the protective love of powerful beings like the Lady of the Lake, love especially intense between leader and men, especially resilient between brothers, especially tender between parents and children.
>
> (p. 375)

Just as the romance absorbed many elements of the *chanson de geste*, so it absorbed and used classical epic and biblical history. The allusions may be naïvely undiscriminating, as in the Scottish metrical romance, *Lancelot of the Laik*, where we meet a 'stranger knight', Sir Priamus who is the son of a prince who rebelled against Rome, of the blood of Alexander and Hector of Troy, related also to Judas and Joshua, and heir to Africa. The names here are used like counters and may equally refer to famous figures or obscure knights. Chrétien, in contrast, uses a reference to the *Aeneid* apparently ornamentally in *Erec et Enide*, but implies dramatic analogies to the story he has been telling of Erec's seeming abandonment of Enide. Now that the lovers have been reunited the old tragedy of Dido can become simply the ornate design on the saddle-bows of Enide's palfrey. Pagan, Christian, and classical elements blend easily and unself-consciously in the last lines of *Sir Gawain*. The lords and ladies all agree that they will wear green bands in brotherhood with Sir Gawayne:

> For þat watȝ accorded þe renoun of þe Rounde Table,
> And he honoured þat hit hade evermore after,
> As hit is breued in þe best boke of romaunce.
> þus in Arthurus day þis aunter bitidde,
> þe Brutus bokeȝ þerof beres wyttenesse;
> Sy þen Brutus, þe bolde burne, boȝed hider fyrst,
> After þe segge and þe asaute watȝ sesed at Troye, iwysse,
> > Mony auntereȝ here-biforne
> > Haf fallen suche er þis.
> > Now þat bere þe croun of þorne,
> > He bryng vus to his blysse! AMEN.

HONY SOYT QUI MAL PENCE.

Perhaps as a result of the same power of synthesizing what seem to us to be disparate sources of experience, we find the writers of romance presenting enchantments and wonders with so unamazed and serene a manner that their strangeness is felt only as a kind of calm, diffused through the whole narrative. The 'marvellous' is not crucial in the definition of medieval romance because emotions and everyday activities are perceived by true romance writers as equally marvellous. That exclamatory searching after novel sensations which we see in the eighteenth-century Gothic is not yet necessary.

Let us see how the 'marvellous' is treated in the following

passage from Chrétien's *Le Chevalier de la Charrete*, or *Lancelot*. Lancelot and his companions find themselves shut in by a series of portcullises in an enemy castle:

> mes cil don plus dire vos doi
> avoit un anel an son doi
> don la pierre tel force avoit
> qu'anchantemanz ne le pooit
> tenir, puis qu'il l'avoit veüe.
> L'anel met devant sa veüe,
> s'esgarde la pierre, et si dit:
> 'Dame, dame, se Dex m'aït,
> or avroie je grant mestier
> que vos me poïssiez eidier.'
> Cele dame une fee estoit
> qui l'anel doné li avoit,
> et si le norri an s'anfance;
> s'avoit an li molt grant fïance
> que ele, an quel leu que il fust,
> secorre et eidier li deüst;
> mes il voit bien a son apel
> et a la pierre de l'anel,
> qu'il n'i a point d'anchantemant,
> et set trestot certainnemant
> qu'il sont anclos et anserré. (ll 2335–55)

(But he, of whom I have more to tell, wore upon his finger a ring, whose stone was of such virtue that any one who gazed at it was freed from the power of enchantment. Holding the ring before his eyes, he gazed at it, and said: 'Lady, lady, so help me God, now I have great need of your succour!' This lady was a fairy, who had given it to him, and who had cared for him in his infancy. And he had great confidence that, wherever he might be, she would aid and succour him. But after appealing to her and gazing upon the ring, he realizes that there is no enchantment here, but that they are actually shut in and confined.)

(Tr. W. W. Comfort, Everyman Edition, London, 1914)

Isolated from its context, the incident is poised between comedy and terror. In context, though these effects are still there, the account runs smoothly on past what appears to be a major crisis and a betrayal of Lancelot by the supernatural powers. He and his companions are left to fight their way out of the castle on their own. Magic is fitful; human action and emotion is Chrétien's permanent resource – as it is of the Gawain poet and Chaucer. An effect of enchantment is most often achieved with purely human forces.

One method of disengaging us from our ordinary assumptions is the swift smooth elision from adventure to adventure. The lack of causal links is again typical of much oral literature or literature based on an oral tradition. What matters artistically, however, is the range of effects which the romance writers create by such means. Such meaningful disconnections are recognizable from our own dream lives. The effect in the romances is to alleviate our concern for individual characters, while at the same time enmeshing us ever more completely in the complexity of the narrative world. At the same time, infinity is suggested by the unfailing appearance of new twists of plot, new messengers, new stories. A little later in *Lancelot*, for instance, Lancelot is engaged in impassioned dialogue with a knight he has just conquered – the same knight who earlier had shamed and mocked him. Should he now force the knight to ride in the cart of ignominy? The knight begs him to kill him rather than shame him.

> Que que cil merci li demande,
> a tant ez vos, par mi la lande,
> une pucele l'anbleüre
> venir sor une fauve mure,
> desafublee et deslïee; ... (ll 2779–83)

(While he is thus beseeching him, behold across the field a maiden riding on a tawny mule, her head uncovered and her dress disarranged.)   (Tr. Comfort)

All attention is suddenly engrossed by the approach of the maiden. The action is momentarily stilled, only to move on with increased impetus as she unexpectedly demands the head of the knight. The change from dialogue to description draws us back into the role of silent spectators and allows our sympathies to shift without pain.

The romances lead us through a complex maze of adventure; but they do not provoke the disagreeable anxiety of a maze. Almost always they have a happy ending. The happy ending has remained typical of romance. This is perhaps one reason why *Troilus and Criseyde* is often claimed as a novel rather than a romance. Romance is an inclusive mode. It offers comedy; it includes suffering. Yet it does not have the concentration of comedy or the finality of tragedy. It celebrates – by the processes of its art as much as by the individual stories – fecundity, freedom and survival.

The enclosed bower, the pleasure dome, the pastoral world, all project images of bliss in which emotional and natural life find repose. Towards the end of *Cligés*, Fenice comes out of the tower, where she has been enclosed for more than a year, into a garden. 'In the middle of the garden stood a grafted tree loaded with blooming flowers and leaves, and with a wide-spreading top. The branches of it were so trained that they all hung downwards until they almost touched the ground; the main trunk, however, from which they sprang rose straight into the air.' Fenice lies within this enclosure, within a walled garden connected to the tower, her lover by her side. The warm, withdrawn, paradisal solitude of the lovers within the branches gives powerful expression to that impulse towards passivity felt throughout the romances. In *The Faerie Queene* Spenser showed how such enclosed and quietist images of bliss (of which one could cite Elizabethan examples from Nashe's *The Unfortunate Traveller* and Sidney's *Arcadia*) can also become the cave of despair:

> Sleepe after toyle, port after stormie seas,
> Ease after warre, death after life does greatly please.

The Bower of Blisse in Spenser's work is infinitely seductive, but delusory and distorting to true human aspirations.

Such images point also towards the artistic weaknesses of the romances when they are not sustained by the tension of genius: their laxity and self-indulgence, their ready procession of accepted formulae. Chaucer pinpoints the follies of romance clichés with comic precision in his burlesque Sir Thopas:

> Sire Thopas fil in love-longynge,
> Al whan he herde the thrustel synge,
>   And pryked as he were wood. [mad]
> His faire steede in his prikynge
> So swatte that men myghte him wrynge;
>   His sydes were al blood.
>
> Sire Thopas eek so wery was
> For prikyng on the softe gras,
>   So fiers was his corage,
> That doun he leyde him in that plas
> To make his steede som solas,
>   An yaf hym good forage. . . .
>
> 'An elf-queene wol I love, ywis,
> For in this world no womman is
>   Worthy to be my make [mate]
>   In towne;
> Alle othere wommen I forsake,
> And to an elf-queene I me take
>   By dale and eek by downe!

The satire works on two levels: mockery of the romance hero's pretensions, and burlesque of the verse conventions. Sir Thopas's sense of special destiny ('in this world no womman is/Worthy to be my make') is paralleled by the tired hyperbole of the description of his horse. Chaucer mocks the travel-weariness of the knight as he wanders aimlessly across the country ('so wery ... For prikyng

on the softe gras'); the contrast between 'So fiers was his corage,/
That doun he leyde him' catches the disparity often half felt
between heroic assertions and actions. The poem is just over two
hundred lines long, yet a full-scale description of the dressing of
Sir Thopas occupies five stanzas, whereas only three stanzas are
needed to dispatch the one piece of action; Sir Thopas's battle with
the giant Sir Oliphant absurdly dissolves just as the climax
approaches:

> Sire Thopas drow abak ful faste;
> This geant at hym stones caste
>   Out of a fel staf-slynge.
> But faire escapeth child Thopas,
> And al it was thurgh Goddes gras,
>   And thurgh his fair berynge.

The evasive formulae avoid any concretely presented action.
The host eventually stops the poet, cursing the 'rym'. 'Rym', in
the sense of verse technique, is indeed Chaucer's chief object of
mockery; the padding which attempts to make clichés sound
meaningful ('By dale and eek by downe') while really only
ensuring the correct number of feet to the line; the bathetic
descent from 'in this world' to 'in towne' for the sake of a rhyme
with 'by downe'. The slack monotony of such devices represents
the lack of artistic concentration with which many English
romance writers handled chivalric themes. Chaucer himself showed
what an artist could make of the romance, both in its traditional
form in the Knightes Tale, and richly and originally in *Troilus and
Criseyde*, the great poem where, as W. P. Ker wrote in *Epic and
Romance*, 'medieval romance passes out of itself'.

ELIZABETHAN ROMANCE

The strong emblematic power of the romance genre tended to
protect unskilled practitioners. Yet the ideal world of the romances

can only find meaningful form through creative precision just because it is ideal. Unless the romance includes a robust particularity there is something specious, something too easily claimed, about its appeal. It resolves into emblems of desire. There is nothing inimical to serious art in the wish to escape the common conditions of life. But wish-fulfilment must be fully, kinetically, acted out with all its attendant pain within the work of art, not proffered like sweetmeats. The suspicion that the romance world is essentially a lie – not only because it is unhistorical but because it is not equivalent to the actual world and not realizable within it – underlies much renaissance and post-renaissance criticism of the form.

But Elizabethan critics were concerned particularly by the sheer popularity of the form. It must be emphasized that the word 'romance' in the sixteenth century could be used for any kind of secular story in verse or prose. The word reaches its widest spectrum of meaning at this period and it is consequently difficult to use it as a defining or characterizing term; we can, however, usefully distinguish its varieties. The principal sources for Elizabethan romance were the chivalric matter of medieval courtly romance; the vast store of classical legends which had become familiar through the new classical learning; these same legends, translated and transformed by way of Italian and French versions; the Italian 'romantic epic'; folk-tale; history. The appetite for stories is shown in the jest-books which reflect popular verbal folk tales, books like *A Hundred Merry Tales* (1526), *The Merry Tales of Skelton* (1566–9), *Tarlton's Jests* (before 1592), and *The Merry Conceited Jests of George Peele* (1607). William Painter's *The Palace of Pleasure* (1566–7) offers a great collection of tales culled mostly from immediate French and Italian sources – which were themselves often based on classical authors.

Any reader who would like to know the sort of stories that the middle-class pre-Shakespearean reader was brought up on can find a delightful account in *Captain Cox, his Ballads and Books; or*

Robert Laneham's Letter (ed. F. J. Furnivall, London, 1871). Laneham himself says: 'Stories I delight in, the more ancient and rare, the more likesume untoo me.' In his account of the entertainment of Queen Elizabeth at Kenilworth in 1575 he describes one of the participants, Captain Cox, a mason from Coventry, and lists his collection of books, plays, and ballads. Immediately striking is the extent to which the chivalric romance predominates among Captain Cox's books: King Arthurz book, Huon of Burdeaus, the squyre of lo degrée, The foour Sons of Aymon, Syr Eglamoour, Syr Tryamoour – such are the names which appear in the list. And Thomas Nashe in his *The Anatomie of Absurditie* mentions many of the same works (which, he hints, are papistical):

> What els I pray you doe these bable bookemungers endevor but to repaire the ruinous wals of Venus Court, to restore to the worlde that forgotten Legendary licence of *lying*, to imitate a fresh the fantasticall dreames of those exiled Abbie-lubbers, from whose idle-pens proceeded those worne out impressions of the feyned no where acts of Arthur of the rounde table, Arthur of little Brittaine, Sir Tristram, Hewon of Burdeaux, the Squire of low degree, the foure sons of Ammon, with infinite others.

Broadly it seems to be true that the matter of the medieval romances has now become part of the popular tradition and, as Laneham's equivocal account of the ancient minstrel and his solemn song suggests, somewhat old-fashioned. Romances based on classical and Italian sources are a newer middle- and upper-class fashion. Ascham called *Morte D'Arthure* a book of 'bold bawdry' but he exclaimed at Painter's *Palace of Pleasure*: 'Ten Morte D'Arthures do not the tenth part so much harm as one of these books made in Italy and translated in England.'

The chivalric romance survived in a different guise in its use as material for pageants and shows: it is likely that the 'great house' romance of Sidney's *Arcadia* as well as the ceremonial allegory in Spenser's *The Faerie Queene* drew upon this fashion.

On Queen Elizabeth's visit to Kenilworth she was conducted by trumpeters:

> Theese armonious blasterz . . . had this muzik meintained from them very delectably while her highness all along this tiltyard rode unto the inner gate next the base coourt of the Castl: where the Lady of the Lake (famous in King Arthurz book) with too nymphes waiting uppon her, arrayed all in sylks, attending her highness comming: from the midst of the Pool, whear, upon a moouabl Iland, bright blazing with torches, she, floting to land, met her Maiesty with a well penned meter and matter after this sort.
>
> *(Captain Cox,* p. 6)

The emblematic splendour of this tableau is followed by some curious raillery between the Queen and the Lady of the Lake – who claims dominion.

This playfulness in the midst of splendour penetrates into the work of Sidney and Spenser, harmonizing with the grave exploration of the nature of nobility in *Arcadia* and *The Faerie Queene*. The serene lightness and thoughtfulness of the Elizabethan courtly romance was partly learned from Ariosto, who had taken the Arthurian material and treated it with a kind of serious disengagement in *Orlando Furioso. The Faerie Queene* is not a 'romance' of the medieval chivalric type: it is too allegorically and ideologically organized for that. Nor is it 'romance' of the simple story-telling variety. Yet it has the characteristics of the romance world and is clearly drawing on a strongly felt native romance tradition sophisticated by familiarity with the Italian 'romantic epic'. There has been much discussion among critics about the degree to which the earlier romances, and particularly Malory, influenced the creation of the poem. For a full discussion of the connections with earlier romances, and particularly the role of Arthur in the poem, the reader can consult Warton's *Observations on the Faerie Queene* (1762) and recent books such as John Arthos, *On the Poetry of Spenser and the Form of Romances*, Josephine Bennett, *The Evolution of the Faerie Queene*, and Rosemond Tuve,

Allegorical Imagery. The central point which emerges from the discussion is that the romances were so accepted as part of the literary tradition that, despite the stringencies of Elizabethan critics, they could still be quite unanalytically invoked and used.

They were seen as a part of the rough substance of life. Sidney, in *An Apologie for Poetry*, declared, ' . . . Poetry is the companion of Camps. I dare undertake, Orlando Furioso, or honest King Arthur, will never displease a soldier.' And in an age which saw literature as a form of activity, the story world of the romances was delighted in for its variety and for the great range of human behaviour exhibited. 'Truly,' wrote Sidney elsewhere in the *Apologie*, 'I have known men, that even with reading *Amadis de Gaule* (which God knoweth wanteth much of a perfect poesy) have found their hearts moved to the exercise of courtesy, liberality, and especially courage.' Sidney's back-handed compliment praises the power of *Amadis* to move men to noble action. His own romance *Arcadia* offers a mirror of nobility. In both Spenser and Sidney the idealization instructs, rather than allowing the reader a complete escape from his own world. Their ideal worlds provide a touchstone for experience.

We can see this 'instructive' function even in the pastoralism of *Arcadia*. The pastoral easily shifts into the political, for a fair landscape implies good government and peace while a ravaged land shows the decay of order and civilization. Thus the dream-like perfection of the Arcadian landscape suggests a perfectly attuned society:

There were hilles which garnished their proud heights with stately trees: humble valleis, whose base estate semed comforted with refreshing of silver rivers: medows, enameld with al sorts of ey-pleasing floures: thickets, which being lined with most pleasant shade, were witnessed so to by the cheerful deposition of many wel-tuned birds: each pasture stored with sheep feeding with sober security, while the prety lambs with bleting oratory craved the dams comfort:

here a shepheards boy piping, as though he should never be old: there a yong shepherdesse knitting, and withall singing, and it seemed that her voice comforted her hands to work, and her hands kept time to her voices musick. (I, 2)

Order, harmony and hierarchy are implicit in this landscape whose values are epitomized in 'knitting and singing'. In the course of the romance we see the ideal landscape ravaged by civil war, the utopian state for a time destroyed.

At the end of Book Three of *The Faerie Queene* the false ideal of Cupid is expressed through mask and show, in a procession that reminds one both of *The Romaun of the Rose* and of the scene at Kenilworth quoted earlier. Against this is set the true image of love in the silent reunion of Amoret and Scudamour. (The stanza below appears only in the first edition):

> Lightly he clipt her twixt his armes twaine,
>   And streightly did embrace her body bright,
>   Her body, late the prison of sad paine,
>   Now the sweet lodge of loue and deare delight:
>   But she faire Lady ourcommen quight
>   Of huge affection, did in pleasure melt,
>   And in sweete rauishment pourd out her spright:
>   No word they spake, nor earthly thing they felt,
> But like two senceles stocks in long embracement dwelt.

This noble reciprocity in love is one of the ideals also in the *Arcadia* where the life the four lovers are seeking to reach is imaged in the marriage of Parthenia and Argalus: 'A happy couple, he joying in her, she joying in her selfe, but in her selfe because she enjoyed him: both encreasing their riches by giving to each other; each making one life double, because they made a double life; one where desire never wanted satisfaction, nor satisfaction ever bred satiety.' (III, 12)

The language of the passages quoted, and particularly that of Sidney, points to the inherent and special ideal of Elizabethan courtly romance. In Lyly's *Euphues* we meet a form of romance in which language has itself become the work's ideal and largely displaced conduct. Sidney's grave authoritative analysis of his characters and their relationships throughout *Arcadia* uses an intricate refinement similar to Lyly's style, but conduct remains the central concern – as it had been in the finest medieval romances. The Elizabethan 'courtly' romance refines and intensifies the ideals of love and honour: it honours its own processes through its creation of a heightened vernacular, capable of articulating nobility. The romance *was*, historically, the vernacular, and the vernacular was conceived as an ideal by the Elizabethans. Moreover, the Spenserian stanza formally expresses the controlled intricacy of romance.

I have emphasized the extent to which the apparently circumscribed worlds of Elizabethan courtly romance bear directly upon life, and upon the conduct of life, even beyond their own age. But I do not want to suggest that they are entirely solemn in their purposes and achievement. They create linguistically poised and brilliant modes of life in which we are flatteringly allowed to share. They bestow upon us a grace and refinement, creating a witty adroitness which comes directly from the experience of reading. They free and perfect us. In this sense too, the romance world keeps its promises and offers us life transfigured: our world is brazen, but the poets deliver a golden.

Although they lived so firmly within its ambience, neither Spenser nor Shakespeare ever used the word 'romance'. It is later critics who have called Shakespeare's last plays his 'romances'. Shakespeare drew on Elizabethan romances for his sources, certainly: Greene's *Pandosto* lies behind *The Winter's Tale* and John Danby persuasively suggests links between the *Arcadia* and *Pericles* in his chapter, 'Sidney and the Late-Shakespearean Romance'. (*Poets on Fortune's Hill*, London, 1952.) Danby makes the crucial point that 'Shakespeare is responding

richly – and with almost lyrical excitement – to the inward theme
of the Romance.'

It is the inwardness that is important: the externals alone would
never explain either Shakespeare's excitement or the individuality of
his accent even when he is handling material that might otherwise
be dismissed as merely conventional or in the sources.

Shakespeare penetrates to the organic patterns celebrated in
romance: the patterns of suffering and survival, of regeneration,
of the pastoral, of the sensuous present eternally fleeting by, of
wish-fulfilment which can create a new world in its own image, the
intricate harmony of chance and time. In the romance nothing is
ever abandoned past recovery; resurgence is always possible.
Shakespeare gives full human form to the truths first expressed
through the narrative patterns of medieval romance.

3

*Cervantes to the
Gothic Novel: The romance and
the rise of the novel*

DON QUIXOTE

The publication of Cervantes's *Don Quixote* and its translation into
English is a major watershed in the history of the romance. In *The
Knight of the Burning Pestle*, a year or so earlier, Beaumont and
Fletcher exploited the absurd disproportion between the old ideal
of chivalric romance and the practice of modern everyday life.
They set up the contrast in class terms, making a joke out of the
citizen's ignorance of theatrical convention as well as the mock-
heroic notion of a grocer transformed into a knight. The idea gave
them the opportunity for exuberant comedy and some pithy
social comment:

> *Rafe*: And certainely those Knights are much to be commended,
> who neglecting their possessions, wander with a Squire and a Dwarfe
> through the Desarts to relieve poore Ladies.
> *Wife*: I by my faith are they, Rafe, let 'em say what they will, they
> are indeed, our Knights neglect their possessions well enough, but
> they do not the rest.

But their handling of the idea was limited, partly because they
treat the idiom of chivalric romance as absurd throughout, and
partly because they are juggling a host of other notions within
the confines of a short play.

In *Don Quixote* Cervantes wrote a work which has all the

amplitude and variety of romance; he respects the mode even while he looks beyond the traditional confines of its subject-matter to new reaches of experience. In the traditional romance no one is ever disillusioned. Disillusionment calls into question the whole wish-fulfilling function of the form and undermines the fabric of its world. Prospero abandoned ceremonial, magic and identity together, in the final maturing declaration which renounces all but the human cycle: 'Our revels now are ended.' But *The Tempest* does not depend upon the romance, or upon the fulfilment of wishes – though most of them are granted. The ordinary world is the distant and desired land to which the characters sail away.

With Cervantes we reach a writer who takes the terms of romance and holds them in tension with the observable facts of life in such a way that a new imaginative pattern emerges which can include, simultaneously, wonder and disillusionment. In *The Sense of an Ending* (New York, 1967) Frank Kermode dates the centrality of the novel from Cervantes:

> It happens that in our phase of civility, the novel is the central form of literary art. It lends itself to explanations borrowed from any intellectual system of the universe which seems at the time satisfactory. Its history is an attempt to evade the laws of what Scott called 'the land of fiction' – the stereotypes which ignore reality, and whose remoteness from it we identify as absurd. From Cervantes forward it has been, when it has satisfied us, the poetry which is 'capable', in the words of Ortega, 'of coping with present reality'. But it is a 'realistic poetry' and its theme is, bluntly, 'the collapse of the poetic' because it has to do with 'the barbarous, brutal, mute, meaningless reality of things'. It cannot work with the old hero, or with the old laws of the land of romance; moreover, such new laws and customs as it creates have themselves to be repeatedly broken under the demands of a changed and no less brutal reality. 'Reality has such a violent temper that it does not tolerate the ideal even when reality itself is idealized.'

Don Quixote is in these terms the first victim of 'the collapse of the poetic'.

Much earlier in its history the romance had survived translation from verse into prose; its ideal vision remained intact. There is always something slightly false in arguments about ideality and reality in medieval literature, because it seems clear that there was no such fixed polarity in medieval thinking. With the beginning of the seventeenth century, however, we are reaching a period in which a conscious opposition is felt between the two: we can see it at work also in the metaphysical poets. Yet in Cervantes's fiction, the ideal world of romance is by no means entirely undermined by reality. It provides both the work's narrative form and much of its imaginative energy. Don Quixote is the most famous victim of the deluding power of romance. He falls totally under its spell. Instead of being content passively to enjoy its ideal world within the quietness of his imagination, he tries to act it out in the recalcitrant everyday world. He believes everything he has read in the romances; he has been so persuaded by the eternal present of romance that he believes it to be actually here and now. He trusts his inward vision more than he trusts his own eyes.

Mimesis is, in this great work, a two-way process. Don Quixote's adventures make it clear that the terms and conditions of chivalric romance rarely engage directly with ordinary experience. But the book also demonstrates that the transfiguring imagination can force the world to imitate its perceptions; imagination need not always mimic external reality. Dulcinea is the 'princesse lointaine' as well as a common wench – because Don Quixote has made her so. When he attacks the windmills he believes himself to be attacking giants: his courage is real, but at the same time its monstrous disproportion casts an ironic light upon the 'heroic' ideal. The balance constantly shifts between the claims of the ideal and the actual.

In the second part, published ten years after the first in reply to spurious continuations, all the characters at the Duke's court have

D

read the famous adventures of Don Quixote. By this stroke
Cervantes brings his hero (still clinging to his anachronistic
chivalric ideal drawn from the romances) into the centre of reality.
The Duke and Duchess set out to convince him that his delusions
are truth and to that end transform their court into a romance
world. Don Quixote's power is such that he can now actually
make the world about him ape his dreams – though, of course, the
Duke imagines himself to be in control of the joke. Yet Don
Quixote is not at home in the court: some distillation of his
imagination's world has escaped them.

Don Quixote is mad; he reaches sanity only when his delusions
have been so encroached upon and undermined that he can no
longer sustain them. He then retires to his bed and dies; they had
become the substance of his life and he cannot survive them.
Cervantes announced his work as an attempt to explode the chivalric romances. And however fully we sympathize with the insights
of madness, it would be sentimental to stress only the creative power
of Don Quixote himself at the expense of the declared burlesque
constructed by Cervantes.

Don Quixote represents the idealization of the self, the refusal
to doubt inner experience, the tendency to base any interpretation
of the world upon personal will, imagination and desire, not upon
an empirical and social consensus of experience. This idealization
of self is bequeathed by the romances to the Romantic poets. One
might claim Don Quixote, in his imaginative isolation, as a fore-
runner of the Romantic hero for whom the external world is
meaningful only in terms of the individual imagination. In debate
with Don Diego de Miranda Don Quixote loftily quenches all
argument. Speaking of the histories of knights-errant being
fictitious Don Diego asks: 'But, does anyone doubt such histories
are false?' 'I doubt it,' answered Don Quixote, 'and let the matter
rest there.' (II, 16)

Don Quixote is probably the single most influential work in the history of the novel. Cervantes's most telling stroke of genius was to embody in his two main characters, Don Quixote and Sancho Panza, the two permanent and universal impulses of fiction. Quixote presents the imagination cut loose from the world of sense and observation, aspiring towards the ideal. This way leads to madness, and to the noble simplification and suggestiveness of myth. Sancho Panza is preoccupied with registering the everyday signs and accepting their authority. His robust life is practicable only in relation to ordinary satisfactions and achievements. Yet Quixote must eat and drink, suffer imprisonment and blows, recognize the obduracy of matter. Sancho, for his part, leaves his family and sets off on a journey of unknown length with Don Quixote on the promise of the governorship of an unknown (and, as it happens, imaginary) island. They are necessary to each other. They interpret the world for each other. They illustrate the interdependence of the impulse to imitate and the impulse to idealize.

Cervantes was able to suggest this balance and interplay partly because, despite his healthy mistrust of the fantasy of chivalric romance, he still took for granted romance-methods of plot construction: he uses interlinked proliferating episodes in which themes apparently long since relinquished recur after hundreds of pages. He cross-cuts incidents; he interpolates stories told by the characters; he shows his knight ambling towards infinity.

In the book, the best-known attack on the chivalric romances is put into the mouth of the Canon. And although it would be a mistake to take this passage as summarizing Cervantes's own aims and perceptions it is worth quoting at some length, both for its characterization of romance and for the way it sets down the paths along which much later criticism of the romance was to run. The Canon admits to having been 'led away with an idle and false Pleasure, to read the Beginnings of almost as many of 'em as have been Printed', but 'I could never yet persuade myself to go through with any one to the End'. Despite this supercilious claim, he goes on to discuss the relationship of parts to the whole:

> Now what Beauty can there be, or what Proportion of the Parts of the Whole, or the Whole to the several Parts, in a Book, or Fable, where a Stripling of Sixteen Years of Age at one Cut of a Sword cleaves a Giant, as tall as a Steeple, through the Middle, as easily as if he were made of Paste-Board? ... And what shall we say of the great Ease and Facility with which an absolute Queen or Empress casts herself into the Arms of an Errant and unknown Knight? ... If it shou'd be answer'd, That the Persons who compose these Books, write them as confess'd Lies; and therefore are not oblig'd to observe Niceties, or to have regard to Truth; I shall make this Reply, That Falshood is so much the more commendable, by how much it more resembles Truth; and is the more pleasing the more it is doubtful and possible. Fabulous Tales ought to be suited to the Reader's Understanding, being so contrived, that all Impossibilities ceasing, all great Accidents appearing feasible and the Mind wholly hanging in Suspence, they may at once surprize, astonish, please and divert; so that Pleasure and Admiration may go hand in hand. ... I have not seen any Book of Knight-Errantry that composes an entire Body of a Fable with all its Parts, so that the Middle is answerable to the Beginning, and the End to the Beginning and Middle; but on the contrary, they form them of so many Limbs, that they rather seem a Chimaera or Monster, than a well-proportion'd Figure. Besides all this, their Stile is uncouth, their Exploits incredible, their Love immodest, their Civility impertinent, their Battles tedious, their Language absurd, their Voyages preposterous; and in short, they are altogether void of solid Ingenuity, and therefore fit to be banish'd a Christian Commonwealth as useless and prejudicial.
>
> (Part I, Book IV, ch. 20, Motteaux's translation)

The shades of Plato and Aristotle move through this typically Renaissance piece of criticism. His aesthetic objections are chiefly to the disproportion of the romances, and their failure to persuade the reader to suspend disbelief. It is the second charge which is the more damaging. In *Don Quixote* itself Cervantes demonstrates how to make fiction resemble truth in such a way that impossibilities cease to be felt as impossible and the free imagination constantly takes on body and significance.

The central delight of the romance is *admiratio*, which Motteaux somewhat slackly renders as admiration. *Admiratio* combines liberating surprise and an exhilarating consciousness of the author's control. If we are to experience surprise we must believe what we are told. (*Admiratio* was also a technique of religious rhetoric.) Cervantes's 'ingenious invention' allows Don Quixote to create the only possible answer to the Canon's charges. Don Quixote begins in the language of criticism, pointing out the historicity of the romance method: its way of 'setting down the Father, Mother, Country, Kindred, Age, Place, and Actions to a tittle, and Day by Day'. But gradually his critical account begins to take on substance and become the story, and we find ourselves transported from debate to enchantment, wandering with his Knight-Errant (so promptly conjured up) through an intricately real castle which surrounds us *now* as we read.

As for Instance, pray tell me, can there be any thing more delightful, than to read a lively Description, which, as it were, brings before your Eyes the following Adventure? A vast lake of boiling Pitch, in which an infinite Multitude of Serpents, Snakes, Crocodiles, and other Sorts of fierce and terrible Creatures, are swimming and traversing backwards and forwards, appears to a Knight-Errant's Sight. [A voice speaks to him from the lake charging him to show his valour and attain bliss. He plunges in and finds himself 'on a sudden in the midst of verdant Fields'. He wanders through a paradisal garden until he reaches a castle 'whose Walls are of massy Gold, the Battlements of Diamonds, and the Gates of Hyacinths'. Many ladies attend him.] What a Sight is it, when in the next Place they lead him into another Room of State, where he finds the Tables so orderly cover'd, that he is surpriz'd and astonish'd? There they pour over his Hands, Water distill'd from Amber and odoriferous Flowers: He is seated in an

Ivory Chair; and while all the Damsels that attend him observe a profound Silence, such variety of Dainties is serv'd up, and all so incomparably dress'd, that his Appetite is at a stand, doubting on which to satisfy its Desire; at the same time his Ears are sweetly entertain'd with Variety of excellent Musick, none perceiving who makes it, or from whence it comes. But above all, what shall we say to see, after the Dinner is ended, and Tables taken away, the Knight left leaning back in his Chair, perhaps picking his Teeth, as is usual; and then another Damsel, much more beautiful than any of the former, comes unexpectedly into the Room, and sitting down by the Knight, begins to inform him what Castle that is, and how she is inchanted in it; with many other Particulars, which surprize the Knight, and astonish those that read his History.   (I, IV, 23)

And, with that, we find ourselves again outside the fictive castle, reading the history, yet still within that larger world of Cervantes's creation. Just as the Canon's account summarizes the critical objections to the romance, so Don Quixote's story (from which I have had space for only a short extract) enacts the power of romance. Its immediacy comes from the senses, which are all in turn aroused. It comes too from its particularity, its occasional familiar improvisation ('perhaps picking his Teeth, as is usual'), and from the processional invocation of ideal narrative motifs: the perilous journey to the enchanted castle, the feast of delights, the new story burgeoning out of his story.

Don Quixote's story shows the triumph of the imagination as it changes the general account into something living, palpable and personally experienced. It is this which gives moral substance to his grandiose witness a few lines later: 'since my being a Knight-Errant, I am brave, courteous, bountiful, well-bred, generous, civil, bold, affable, patient, a Sufferer of Hardships, Imprisonment and Inchantments'. There is absurdity in this – as in his story – but there is also a noble delight and confidence. The marvellous control and freedom of Cervantes's handling of the episode make it (surely deliberately) an exemplum of the special excellence the

Canon had allowed to romance: the opportunity it affords for a gifted intellect to display itself.

In *Don Quixote* Cervantes succeeds in overarching the romance and reaching beyond it to include other modes of fiction. His hero, unlike the traditional knight of romance, makes his will and dies in his bed. The illusions of life can end only with death because they inform all our perceptions. The book ends with a last juggling of fictive truth and fictive illusion; Cervantes speaks in the person of *Cid Hamet Benengeli:* 'For me alone was Don Quixote born, and I for him; it was his to act; mine to write; we two together make but one.' *Don Quixote* brings home the extent to which all good fiction must partake of the qualities of romance: fiction creates a coherent illusion; it creates an absorbing imaginative world composed of particulars seen with an intensity which suggests the ideal; it is sustained by the subjective imagination of the writer. At the most general and permanent level it is probably more accurate to see the realistic novel as a mutation of the romance rather than as replacing it.

THE DECLINE OF THE ROMANCE

In the very early days of the courtly romance it spoke far more directly to people's experience than did the classical literature of the learned; in the late seventeenth and early eighteenth centuries, however, courtly romance receded for a time into a remote, highly stylized world almost unrecognizably distant from actual approachable experience. Neo-classical thought and forms now answered to the temper of the age. We can see the process of withdrawal beginning already, perhaps, in the leisurely, playful, aristocratic tone of the *Arcadia* with its *roman à clef* allusions comprehensible only to an inner group. It is far more striking in the French seventeenth-century romances which remained fashionable in England into the eighteenth century. Honoré d'Urfée's *L'Astrée* (which appeared at roughly the same time as

Don Quixote in five instalments between 1607 and 1619) has a precious, undulating narrative line; its delights emerge from its neo-platonic pastoralism. The most influential of the French Romances in England was perhaps *Le Grand Cyrus*, with its emphasis on prowess and honour. It set the tone for the 'heroic' preoccupations of the later seventeenth century. These seventeenth-century prose romances draw heavily upon the 'romantic epics' of Ariosto and Tasso which combine elements of the Carolingian *chanson de geste* with the Arthurian romance. The French romances deal in extremes: massive single-handed feats of arms, prodigious coincidences, heightened notions of honour in love:

> But chiefly Love – to Love an Altar built
> Of twelve vast *French* Romances, neatly gilt.
> (*The Rape of the Lock*, 1712, ii, 37–8)

Pope's 'neatly gilt' beautifully captures the element of display and safe frivolity which undermines, if not the works themselves, at least the way they were regarded and used. They were part of the exclusive world of money and leisure.

This may be one reason why Milton, searching for a theme for his great epic enterprise, had turned down his earlier idea of an Arthurian epic.

> Not sedulous by Nature to indite
> Wars, hitherto the only Argument
> Heroic deem'd, chief maistry to dissect
> With long and tedious havoc fabl'd Knights
> In Battles feign'd; the better fortitude
> Of Patience and Heroic Martyrdom
> Unsung; or to describe Races and Games,
> Or tilting Furniture, emblazon'd Shields,
> Impreses quaint, Caparisons and Steeds;
> Bases and tinsel Trappings, gorgeous Knights
> At Joust and Tournament; then marshall'd Feast

Serv'd up in Hall with Sewers, and Seneschals;
The skill of Artifice or Office mean,
Not that which justly gives Heroic name
To Person or to Poem.

(*Paradise Lost*, ix, 27–41)

Milton rejects the 'feign'd' battles, the 'skill of Artifice or Office mean'; he repudiates what he sees as the essential triviality of chivalric concerns, for the true heroic which will often find expression in patience rather than in prowess. He sets himself to describe not just the 'tedious havoc' of fabled knights but the War in Heaven, not merely paradisal gardens of the senses but Paradise itself. When he does so he is not ashamed to draw on language already familiar to us from the chivalric romances.

In a somewhat parallel way, Bunyan in *Pilgrim's Progress* re-interprets motifs from the popular romances in terms of religious allegory. He creates an imaginative synthesis between biblical language and stories and the language and stories of romances such as *Bevis of Southampton* and the *Seven Champions of Christendom*. It has sometimes been suggested that he must have been familiar with the first book of *The Faerie Queene* (though Harold Golder, who made a detailed study of the romance elements in Bunyan, thought this unlikely ('Bunyan and Spenser', *P.M.L.A.*, XLV, 1930)). There are clearly recognizable traditional romance motifs in Apollyon and Giant Despair with his enchanted castle. The delights of the House Beautiful are reached only by a treacherous path up a steep hill. (Don Quixote's knight plunged into the boiling lake to reach his blissful castle.) The Delectable Mountains are peopled with pastoral shepherds. The secular romance has been taken over and interpreted into religious experience. The link between romance and religion had been earlier established in the Grail legends; to the Puritan writers the romance is simply a tool, something to be used and grown beyond, on the path to religious knowledge.

At the end of the seventeenth century, prose romance survives in three forms: in the aristocratic French heroic romance, in the Puritan transformation of romance to religious meaning, and in the popular 'criminal romances' on which Defoe was later to draw. The criminal romances gave graphic accounts of the exploits of the underworld and their climax is usually a heroic death-speech before hanging. They illustrate one seemingly paradoxical extension of the romance: stories which the audience must believe actually to have happened if they are to enjoy the excitement and release offered. (The popular magazine, *True Romances*, shows the continuation of this tradition.) These 'criminal romances' dealing always with 'here and now' adventures, act out, imaginatively, wishes that cannot safely be fulfilled in life. Francis Kirkman, author of *The Counterfeit Lady Unveiled*, one of the best known, described himself in his autobiography *The Unlucky Citizen* (1673) as a Don Quixote, always spellbound by romances. Romance changes with its audience: the readers of such works were mostly small traders and other lower-middle-class people who depended on respectability. The criminal romance represents one of the early reconciliations between 'novel' and 'romance'. Defoe's fiction uses the techniques they had developed. Fielding later turned them to his own political account in the mock-heroic *Jonathan Wild*.

By the middle of the eighteenth century the French romances had all the tawdriness of a recently bygone fashion, and the romance form was seen by contemporary writers as a thing of the past. Partly because the romance was an ancient form it was considered to be barbarous, a part of the infancy of the world now replaced by more civilized genres. True, the term 'romance' continued to be used to describe a wide spectrum of prose fiction, particularly the entertaining works of women writers like Eliza Haywood. But the seventeen-forties established the novel of ordinary or domestic life in the work of Richardson and Fielding. In 1750, Dr Johnson wrote in the fourth number of *The Rambler*:

The works of fiction with which the present generation seems more particularly delighted, are such as exhibit life in its true state, diversified only by accidents that daily happen in the world, and influenced by passions and qualities which are really to be found in conversing with mankind.

This kind of writing may be termed not improperly the comedy of romance, and is to be conducted nearly by the rules of comick poetry. Its province is to bring about natural events by easy means, and to keep up curiosity without the help of wonder: it is therefore precluded from the machines and experiments of the heroic romance, and can neither employ giants to snatch away a lady from the nuptial rites, nor knights to bring her back from captivity; it can neither bewilder its personages in deserts, nor lodge them in imaginary castles.

Johnson still uses the term 'romance': the novel is the comedy of romance as opposed to the heroic romance. (The term 'novel' was not generally established until a little later in the century.) To him the 'true state' of life is the daily state and he is puzzled as to why 'this wild strain of imagination found reception so long in polite and learned ages'. The new kind of writing, he asserts, imposes new responsibilities on authors because in the former romances 'the reader was in very little danger of making any applications to himself' (we can contrast Sidney's view of their effectiveness as examples). Now, however, 'an adventurer is levelled with the rest of the world' and 'young spectators hope, by observing his behaviour and success, to regulate their own practices'. This leads Johnson to demand, in effect, that the novel should take on the idealizing function of romance – though he interprets the ideal purely in moral terms: 'In narratives where historical veracity has no place, I cannot discover why there should not be exhibited the most perfect idea of virtue ... Vice, for vice is necessary to be shown, should always disgust.'

What Johnson is demanding would be far closer to the romance characterization of 'types', than anything which the actual later development of the novel produced. This is in part the effect of his neo-classical and his Christian views, but it almost certainly comes from a habit of mind towards fiction which is based on the experience of 'the old romances', however much he may think himself at odds with them. We can see this relationship creatively at work in *Rasselas* which he wrote only a few years later. The whole argument of the book is avowedly anti-ideal; but the Oriental Tale is used homiletically for the structure of the story; he reminds us of the myth of Icarus; his characters are 'types'; he includes one wild adventure – the capture of Pekuah by the Arabs – but he firmly makes it subside into civility. Pekuah has not been raped, though she has been carried off. Her captor has been a gentleman. I feel tempted to see this episode (which runs contrary to the book's general tendency to point out that things are worse than they appear) as Johnson's own form of the romance, in which reason and civilization emerge from apparent barbarity. It is both a burlesque reversal of the common course of such episodes and a civilized wish-fulfilment.

The novel, according to his dictionary, is 'a smooth tale, generally of love'; the romance is 'a military fable of the middle ages; a tale of wild adventures in love and chivalry'. The romance, he suggests, offers an autotelic world, obeying its own laws and only distantly connected to the actual; the novel deals with the everyday. The polarization is exaggerated, even in terms of the novels he had most immediately in mind. *Clarissa* hardly deals with 'accidents that daily happen in the world'. But he has seized upon one essential distinction: the novel can be applied directly, not only symbolically, to ordinary life.

The novel aspires to be a kind of history and a kind of conduct book. The desire to be a kind of history was already there in *Don Quixote* which Cervantes calls a 'historia' – a word which in Spanish can mean both 'story' and 'history'. Fielding in *Tom Jones* speaks quizzically of novelists as 'historical writers who do not draw their material from records' (Book IX, ch. 1). The romance had earlier drawn much of its energy from history: it concentrated on heroic exploits; the novel concentrates on 'social' history. Moreover, as Clara Reeve's Euphues points out in *The Progress of Romance*, even the old romances had turned history into a kind of fiction. The romance concentrates on ideal possibilities; the novel on actual possibilities. Fielding writes of 'foolish novels and monstrous romances'. At this period the exaggeration and remoteness of romance are constantly set in contrast with the immediacy of the novel – however trite and trivial its concerns are felt to be.

In part this was a piece of literary sleight-of-hand by novelists who used it as a means of creating verisimilitude. In *The Female Quixote*, one of the first in the line of anti-romance novels to which Jane Austen's *Northanger Abbey* belongs, Charlotte Lennox traces the fortunes of a young woman whose expectations of life have been largely formed by ill-advised reading in her grandfather's library 'in which, unfortunately for her, were great Store of Romances, and, what was still more unfortunate, not in the original French, but in very bad translations'. .... 'By them she was taught to believe, that Love was the ruling Principle of the World; that every other Passion was subordinate to this; and that it caused all the Happiness and Miseries of Life.'

The romances allowed their readers – who were mainly women – to immerse themselves without responsibility in a hectic world which made real life pale by comparison. The fear that the romance would seduce the imagination, as well as mislead, may have been based on a half-acknowledged recognition that women's lives were very circumscribed in their actual possibilities. The 'marvellous' is mistrusted, partly because it tallies so ill with experience, but, perhaps, even more because coincidence and magic create a kind of pagan freedom far removed from the world of duty. Richardson's triumph as a novelist was his power to release and use psychic extremes without ever losing hold on the responsibilities created by actual life. The 'revolutionary' impulse of romance is stirring in both *Pamela* and *Clarissa*, and harbinges the romantic revival. But it would be unwise to claim either of them as romances in their total effect. Richardson uses romance elements but he places them in relationship to contemporary experience. He recognizes the self-absorption inherent in unmixed romance. Lovelace, who can see himself only through a series of literary poses, likens himself at one point to a romance hero: 'But was ever hero in romance (fighting with giants and dragons excepted) called upon to harder trials?' Richardson goes full circle past romance: in *Pamela* by devoting the second volume to the duties of his heroine's married life; in *Clarissa* by refusing the 'happy ending' of marrying his heroine to her loved seducer and driving the novel on into religious tragedy. In *Sir Charles Grandison* he creates an eighteenth-century version of the perfect knight of chivalry. He is in the Puritan tradition of Milton and Bunyan which can absorb the power of the romance and turn it to religious ends.

Although 'romances' were suspect because their dream worlds seduce and mislead, the generosity of their ideals of love was also recognized. James Fordyce, in his *Sermons to Young Women* (1766) made the point well (this was the volume to which Lydia Bennet failed to attend when it was read aloud by Mr Collins in *Pride and Prejudice*):

> In the old Romance the passion appeared with all its enthusiasm. But then it was the enthusiasm of honour; for love and honour were there the same. The men were sincere, magnanimous and noble; the women were patterns of chastity, dignity, and affection ... The characters they drew were, no doubt, often heightened beyond nature; and the incidents they related it is certain, were commonly blended with the most ridiculous extravagance. At present, however, I believe, they may be read with perfect safety, if indeed there be any who choose to look into them.

The times in which we live are in no danger of adopting a system of romantic virtue.

The romance was seen as a dangerously confusing but not necessarily perverse moral guide. It was also (though this was less discussed) felt to threaten the dominance of reason. In the Preface to *Evelina* (1778) Fanny Burney prepares her readers for disappointment if they hope for the regions 'of *Romance*: where Fiction is coloured by all the gay tints of luxurious Imagination, where Reason is an outcast, and where the sublimity of the *Marvellous* rejects all aid from sober Probability.'

THE GOTHIC REVIVAL

By the time Fanny Burney was writing, a far more immediate threat to reason than the older romances was emerging. It is suggested in that phrase, 'the sublimity of the *Marvellous*'. Clara Reeve's *The Champion of Virtue, or, The Old English Baron* had been published in the previous year with its lost heir and decayed and haunted castle wing. And Clara Reeve was following a fashion begun a decade before with the publication in 1765 of Horace Walpole's *The Castle of Otranto*. The fashion for the Gothic romance had already begun, although Mrs Radcliffe – its most popular author – did not produce her first major novel, *The Mysteries of Udolpho* – until 1794. In 1773 J. and A. L. Aiken (Mrs Barbauld) published an essay on romances and 'On the Pleasure derived from Objects of Terror' (*Miscellaneous Pieces in Prose*). They group the 'old Gothic romance and the Eastern tale' together and they distinguish between two kinds of terror: 'natural terror' which is allied to life and inclined to be painful, and the 'marvellous' which results in an 'artificial terror'. This 'artificial terror' includes wonder, and in it pain is overruled by amazement. The Gothic novelists had rediscovered the power of sensation, which under the names of 'wonder' and 'admiration' had always been part of the pleasure of romance. But now 'sensation' was linked to the grotesque, the sublime, and the supernatural. The 'marvellous' was felt to be threatening.

To the eighteenth-century critics wonders were the 'machinery' of romance. *The Monthly Review* (XXXII, 1765) spoke of the now-popular Gothic fiction 'with its machinery of ghosts and goblins'. This mechanistic view superseded the older serenity in the face of magic, that flexible sense of the possible and the impossible which allowed an allegorical suggestiveness to the medieval romances without the need for a fully allegorized interpretation. Hazlitt neatly pinpointed the fixed, statuesque quality of the marvels in many Gothic novels in his comments on the first of them, Walpole's *The Castle of Otranto* (1765). In *English Comic Writers* (1819), he describes the episode of the great hand and arm thrust into the courtyard, as 'dry, meagre, and without effect'. They 'are the pasteboard machinery of a pantomime; they shock the senses and have no purchase on the imagination. They are a matter-of-fact impossibility: a fixture and no longer a phantom.' He is speaking with all the vision of the intervening Romantic movement behind him and is to that extent unjust to Walpole's effectiveness. But we see the besetting self-consciousness of Gothic novelists in Walpole's apology to the first edition: 'Miracles, visions, necromancy, dreams, and other preternatural events are exploded now, even from romances. That was not the case when our author wrote; much less when the story itself is supposed to have happened.' He appeals to historical accuracy, but his letters make it clear that the inspiration for the book sprang from other sources than remote history.

In a letter to William Cole (9 March, 1765) Walpole said that the romance grew out of a dream he had had and that he wrote it as a relief from politics. *The Castle of Otranto* is at one level a mythic representation of Walpole's political experience. Walpole wrote in another later letter: 'Visions, you know, have always been my pasture; and so far from growing old enough to quarrel with their emptiness I almost think there is no wisdom comparable to exchanging what is called the realities of life for dreams.' Despite its incidental absurdities the Gothic romance is a serious form which freed the primal material of dreams and terrors back into fiction. In the second preface to *Otranto* Walpole suggested that the 'copying of nature' in which novelists of his time excelled meant that 'the great resources of fancy have been dammed up, by a strict adherence to common life'.

With the rise of the Gothic, the floodgates of fancy were opened, and the commitment to *imagination* as the source of inspiration, which reached its fruition among the romantic poets, had begun. Maturin, in *Melmoth the Wanderer* (1820) was to take the form to the degree of introspection where he could write: 'Emotions are my events.' In the Gothic romance, pastoralism changes into gloomy forests and awe-inspiring mountains. The natural scene now represents no sunny ideal of social harmony but the underside of consciousness. Where the individual identity is (in Wordsworth's phrase) 'fostered alike by beauty and by fear'. The characters are types, though there is an increasing analytical subtlety in the form, as a comparison between Mrs Radcliffe's *The Romance of the Forest* and *The Italian* will show. The heroines preserve that incandescent virtue and beauty which invites villainy to attempt their destruction.

This symbolic representation of the good and evil impulses in man's nature reaches a far more disturbing form in one of the last novels of the genre, Mary Shelley's *Frankenstein*, where man's creativity becomes nightmare and unleashes a monster upon the world. The sense of schizophrenia in *Frankenstein* was to be taken up later in the nineteenth century by Robert Louis Stevenson in *Dr Jekyll and Mr Hyde*, and in the detective story with its interdependent hero and villain, such as Sherlock Holmes and Moriarty. But I do not propose to pursue these links further since these later works cannot convincingly be called 'romances'. Nevertheless the Gothic romance did bequeath a powerful strain of psychological fantasy, most telling in Schiller's romances and continuing with particular power in German fiction, which has always accepted romance elements more readily than has the English novel.

Strikingly, some Surrealist writers in the 1920's considered the Gothic novel the only past literature worth reading. This was because of its anti-rational or supra-rational bias. André Breton in the *Manifesto of Surrealism* (1924) sees such work as a deliberate act of anti-rational provocation and he asserts that 'the marvellous alone is capable of bringing fertility to works from an inferior genre like the novel'. And in 'Le Merveilleux contre le mystère' (reprinted in *La Cité des Champs*, Paris, 1953) he says that the surrealist's task is

the elaboration of a *collective myth* suitable to our period for the same reason as . . . the Gothic genre must be considered as pathogronomic of the great social disturbance which took possession of Europe at the end of the eighteenth century.

Breton here seizes upon one of the special strengths of the romance in all its mutations. It offers a peculiarly precise register of the ideals and terrors of the age, particularly those which could find no other form. The romance is mimetic at a mythic level. It forms itself about the collective subconscious of an age. This does not always make it good literature, or good reading in another age, but it means that it is always suggestive; it can allow us to participate dramatically for a time in the distinctive psychic stresses of alien societies. In this way we also become more conscious of the character of our own time.

4
Romanticism
and Post-Romantic Romance

The 'marvellous' seemed to seventeenth- and eighteenth-century critics to be the distinguishing mark of the romance. The Romantic attitude to the romance and its associated forms is distinguished by conscious revivalism – revivalism in both senses of the word, since it is present both as pedantic antiquarianism and as a restoring to spiritual life.

In the previous chapter I have tracked some of the mutations undergone by the prose romance in the eighteenth century. The poetic romance, meanwhile, continued through the form of the popular ballad. The publication, first, of Macpherson's *Ossian* (1760), and then five years later, of Bishop Percy's *Reliques of Ancient English Poetry*, began to create fresh interest in the possibilities of remote non-classical poetic worlds.

THE ROMANCE AND SOME ROMANTIC POEMS

The words 'romance' and 'romantic' are closely connected. In English and German eighteenth-century usage, 'romantic' still means essentially 'something that could happen in a romance' – the equivalent word in French is 'romanesque'. The writers who emerged towards the end of the eighteenth century (the period which is usually taken as the start of the Romantic age in England) perceived that 'what happens in a romance' is not simply unreal or artificial. Rather, it expresses the lost or repressed emotional forces of the imagination, which they sought to release. The Romantic poets found this expressive life in a variety of sources akin to the romance. They found it in ballads, both the popular broadsheet ballads (which are perhaps the principal formal inspiration for Wordsworth's *Lyrical Ballads*) and the traditional border ballads (which lie behind Coleridge's *The Ancient Mariner*). They found it in oriental tales, and especially in *The Arabian Nights*. They found it in the Gothic novel's version of history (Coleridge's *Christabel* draws on this literary tradition). They found it in the Middle Ages. (Schlegel argued that 'romantic' could be applied to any work whose inspiration was medieval rather then classical.) They found it in folk-tale and fairy-tale – this last source is particularly important for German literature and although I am limiting my discussion to English Romantic writers it is worth noting that Schlegel's influential *Brief über den Roman* (*Letter about the Novel*) postulates a form for fiction much closer to the romance than to the realistic novel.

The invocation of 'golden-tongued romance with serene lute', to use Keats's phrase, was one of the great imaginative resources of Romantic and post-Romantic poetry. We can see it in *Kubla Khan* and, equally, in Tennyson's *Idylls of the King*. In both cases, the significance of the poem is felt to depend upon the establishment of an imaginative relationship between the romance world and the poet's own world: for Coleridge, the world of his inner creative life; for the Victorian Tennyson, the whole life of his time. For the poets of the high Romantic period romance was essentially an introspective mode: its pleasure domes and faerie lands were within the mind. The extensive landscapes of medieval and renaissance romance have become *paysages intérieurs*.

In *Kubla Khan* we have one of the richest and noblest expressions of the poet's creative longing to resurrect lost worlds within the imagination. The pleasure-dome built by Kubla Khan is recreated by the poet through sensuous language. We recognize the dome and the method of intense sense-arousal from other romance literature:

> In Xanadu did Kubla Khan
> A stately pleasure-dome decree:
> Where Alph, the sacred river, ran
> Through caverns measureless to man
>   Down to a sunless sea.
> So twice five miles of fertile ground
> With walls and towers were girdled round:
> And here were gardens bright with sinuous rills,
> Where blossomed many an incense-bearing tree;
> And here were forests ancient as the hills,
> Enfolding sunny spots of greenery.

The poet makes afresh this Eastern palace of delights through the eternal present of the senses and of the human body (suggested in words like 'girdled' and 'enfolded' and more emphatically in the language of the second stanza).

In the last stanza the poet seeks synaesthetically to revive not only the picture of the palace but the 'symphony and song' of the 'damsel with a dulcimer', seen once in a vision. This, if recaptured, would free him to make Kubla Khan's kingdom anew, not simply by reviving it, but by transposing it into a new medium: music. It would become 'carmina', with the poet as bard, totally expressive and totally creative, able physically to 'build' the dome through music's vibrations 'in air'.

> Could I revive within me
> Her symphony and song,
>   To such a deep delight 'twould win me,
> That with music loud and long,
> I would build that dome in air,
> That sunny dome! those caves of ice!
> And all who heard should see them there,
> And all should cry, Beware! Beware!
> His flashing eyes, his floating hair!

> Weave a circle round him thrice,
> And close your eyes with holy dread,
> For he on honey-dew hath fed,
> And drunk the milk of Paradise.

'All who heard should see them there': they would become actual through the imaginative authority of the poet's music. As the poem ends, the poet has become part of the exotic visionary world he describes, both hypothetically ('Could I revive') and actually in the imagined cry ('he on honey-dew hath fed'). The process of *Kubla Khan* is typical of romance experience: it converts a hypothetical, contingent and often disordered imaginative world into an actual experience in which, through detail of the senses, we enter a vision both marvellous and concrete. There may well be an intermittent clinical association between romance and drugs, but the more continuous relationship is with the dream-experience which is available to everyone.

In *Kubla Khan* the poet becomes at the end a figure in the poetic landscape. Whereas in the medieval romance the writer is quizzically present, commenting, interpreting, offering asides to the reader, in the Romantic period the poet seeks to be immersed in the same element as the imaginative forms he presents. The medieval romances were extroverted in that they offered ample, thronging and complete social images. This expansiveness is rarely felt among the Romantic poets, partly because of their intensive poetic mode, but partly also because the worlds displayed by the old romances are no longer felt to be fully meaningful in themselves. Their meaning for Coleridge or Keats or even Scott depends upon a perceived relationship with the poet's own imaginative identity.

In *The Eve of St Agnes* Keats created a romance which, without being subjective, is totally conscious. He knits up elements from many stages in the romance's history. The central story could have come from a border ballad; the tradition that a girl can see her future lover on St Agnes' Eve was available from folk-tale; the medievalism (the cobwebs, the stained-glass windows, the ancient retainer, Angela) calls on the Gothic; the stanza form is Spenserian. But the work is not a patchwork: it lives vibrantly in its own created present as Madeline 'Unclasps her warmed jewels one by one' or as the lovers creep through the castle:

> In all the house was heard no human sound.
> A chain-droop'd lamp was flickering by each door;
> The arras, rich with horseman, hawk, and hound,
> Flutter'd in the besieging wind's uproar;
> And the long carpets rose along the gusty floor.

The poem opens in the past tense, 'St Agnes' Eve – Ah, bitter chill it was!' but in the second stanza it changes to the present. This has its effect throughout the poem which, by means of sensuous contrast and rapid changes of scene, maintains its effect of present action. The final stanza draws us up with a deliberate shock as the whole tale reels backwards into the remote past: 'The key turns, and the door upon its hinges groans'.

> And they are gone: aye, ages long ago
> These lovers fled away into the storm.

The force of the word 'gone' shifts from relief (the lovers have escaped), to loss ('ages long ago'). Nightmare, old age, and death complete the human cycle:

> That night the Baron dreamt of many a woe,
> And all his warrior-guests, with shade and form
> Of witch, and demon, and large coffin-worm,
> Were long be-nightmar'd. Angela the old
> Died palsy-twitch'd, with meagre face deform;
> The Beadsman, after thousand aves told,
> For aye unsought-for slept among his ashes cold.

For Keats, Romance is the myth of youth.

Early in the poem he refused to describe the gorgeous social celebrations in order to concentrate on the private world of the two lovers. In doing so, he decisively excludes one of the optimistic purposes of older romance: its expression of communal delight. He speaks of the 'argent revelry' as

> Numerous as shadows haunting faerily
> The brain, new stuff'd, in youth, with triumphs gay
> Of old romance.

The 'triumphs gay' interested Keats less than the coalescence of ideal dream and palpable reality which the lovers experience: 'into her dream he melted.' It is this intensely personal centre to the poem which creates its vital harmony; at the end Keats quietly acknowledges the frailty as well as the resilience of the poem's ideals: the remoteness of the romance world and the fleeting sensuous engrossment of youth and love.

Keats turned away in *The Eve of St Agnes* from the 'argent revelry'. Such social set-pieces were one of the constant motifs of the newly fashionable historic novel. It is arguable how far the historical novel can be seen as descending from the romance tradition. Clearly the Gothic romance had fostered an interest in the trappings of the remote historical past. In the hands of its most creative practitioner, Walter Scott, the historical novel was sprung upon the tension between a nation's past and its modern character. Three years before the publication of *Waverley*, Scott wrote an introduction to Walpole's *The Castle of Otranto* (John Ballantyne's edition of 1811) which suggests something of his views on the relationship between romance and modern novel. Walpole's object, Scott says, was 'to unite the marvellous turn of incident and imposing tone of chivalry, exhibited in the ancient romance, with that accurate display of human character and contrast of feelings and passions which is, or ought to be, delineated in the modern novel ...'

The phrase 'accurate display of human character' pinpoints what Scott felt to be the contrast between the old romances and modern fiction. In his poems, *Marmion*, for example, he is content to continue the idealized simplification of romance-characterization, but in the novel he felt that something more life-size and more complex was required. He found the perspective he was seeking by placing his first novel *Waverley* 'sixty years since', and he explains, quite explicitly, the effect at which he is aiming. He wants to find some permanent ground between the remote picturesqueness of romance and the ephemerality of present-day fashion:

> I would have my readers understand, that they will meet in the following pages neither a romance of chivalry, nor a tale of modern manners; that my hero will neither have iron on his shoulders, as of yore, nor on the heels of his boots, as is the present fashion of Bond Street; and that my damsels will neither be clothed 'in purple and in pall', like the Lady Alice of an old ballad, nor reduced to the primitive nakedness of a modern fashionable at a rout. From this my choice of an era the understanding critic may farther presage, that the object of my tale is more a description of men than manners.

By choosing a neutral, unfashionable period of the recent past he is, he says, deliberately 'throwing the force of my narrative upon the characters and passions of the actors; those passions common to men in all stages of society'. He seems to be working on the neo-classical principle that what is interesting is the *permanent* rather than the temporary impulses of man's nature.

George Lukács in *The Historical Novel* (Tr. H. and S. Mitchell, London, 1962) emphasizes the interaction between individual character and the unity of social existence in Scott's novels. Lukács compares them to the epic, though he carefully distinguishes between epic and novel. 'One common factor is the way in which they both seek to create the impression of life as it normally is *as a whole*.' But in Scott's novels the important features are 'not the supreme manifestations of an essentially unchanging world order (as far as literature is concerned), but on the contrary the radical sharpening of social trends in an historical crisis' (p. 46).

The accuracy of Scott's historicism, his sense of the temper of precise periods and their relationship to the time at which he writes, separates most of his work from the romance tradition. (When that accuracy is missing, as in the work of many later novelists, the historical novel does become a lax type of romance.) Scott makes it clear that periods of the past, whether the period of Cœur de Lion in *Ivanhoe* or of seventeenth-century Scotland in *Old Mortality*, were unideal. Though they differ from our own time they exist on an equivalent scale. Lukács sees 'The Classical Historical Novel in Struggle with Romanticism'; for his arguments I recommend the interested reader to his book. Though one could argue for a direct line of descent from romance to a novel like *The Bride of Lammermoor*, Scott's influence increased the impulse towards *realism* – the unidealized representation of actuality – which culminated, in the middle of the century, in the rich psychological and social patterns of George Eliot's novels.

'REALISM' AND 'ROMANCE'

From the Romantic period onwards writers more and more abandon the article before 'romance'. Romance has become a literary quality rather than a form and it is frequently set against 'reality' in literary argument. At the same time throughout the nineteenth century the idea of 'the romance' was persistently revived and interpreted afresh by artists according to their individual needs. As a result it begins to appear in a bizarre variety of forms: daydream, allegory, history, fairy-tale, horror-tale, psychological fantasy. All could be claimed as romances.

For the Elizabethans, the chivalric romances had provided material for pageants and displays; for the Victorians they provide the subject-matter for art. The Pre-Raphaelite Brotherhood shows the interplay between 'the real' and 'the ideal' at its most aesthetically complex. The early Pre-Raphaelites sought absolute historical and technical accuracy in their depictions, but the accuracy was itself an act of imaginative synthesis since their subject-matter was almost always taken from remote periods and cultures: Holman Hunt and Millais in the eighteen-fifties draw on biblical, Arthurian and historical sources. (Millais's *Sir Isumbras at the Ford* or *A Dream of the Past* (1857) uses Arthurian material from Malory; his earlier *Mariana* transposes the psychological pictorialism of Tennyson's poem on to canvas.) The later heirs of Pre-Raphaelitism invoke the dream of the Middle Ages in both poetry and art. Rossetti and William Morris each create a palpable ideal which turns away from the values of their own society and from its smoky atmosphere towards a world whose complexities they see as being all of the spirit.

Morris's *The Earthly Paradise* (1868–70), gathers up stories from all over the world in such a way that they come to represent the organic cycle of the natural year: a spiritual turning usually disguised by the pall of industrialism. The poem opens:

> Forget six counties overhung with smoke,
> Forget the snorting steam and piston stroke,
> Forget the spreading of the hideous town;
> Think rather of the pack-horse on the down,
> And dream of London, small, and white, and clean,
> The clear Thames bordered by its gardens green; . . .

Morris's offer of escape was not simply an indulgence. It was an act of cleansing. He did not himself forget the life of his times: he sought to change its values. One of the means by which he did this was to recreate various kinds of beauty, using his sources eclectically while at the same time respecting them intrinsically. He was one of the first nineteenth-century translators of old French romances; he made the world of the Icelandic Sagas available through his powerful renderings; in 1877 he translated the *Aeneid*; and a year later he wrote *Sigurd the Volsung* and *The Fall of the Niblungs*.

When he wrote his own utopian critique of English society, *News from Nowhere* (1890), he called upon the idealist techniques he had learned from his reading in romance, allegory, and saga. The chief lesson he had learnt from them was their sensuously complete representation of the ideal – a kind of hyperaesthesia which allows the materials of the world to press directly upon the identity and intensify awareness. His designs create a parallel state of satisfying visual arousal.

Tennyson had perfected the method of descriptive symbolism to create and represent *states of mind* earlier in the century. A poem like *The Lady of Shalott* uses an Arthurian episode to dramatize mythically the tensions between the claims of enclosed and active life, between the creative self and the replenishing world beyond self. His art was essentially psychological. Despite his growing social purposiveness, he did not attempt Morris's active social allegorizing in his invocation of romance material, even in the *Idylls of the King*. Tennyson and Morris are the two poets who re-create the romances in terms which go beyond archaism to become a living idiom of thought.

Whereas poets could call upon romance material intact from other ages, novelists interpreted the word differently. The debate about realism is central to theories of fiction from the eighteen-fifties to eighties in England. Trollope put the dispute at its simplest in a letter to George Eliot in 1853:

> You know that my novels are not sensational. In *Rachel Ray* I have attempted to confine myself absolutely to the commonest details of commonplace life among ordinary people allowing myself no incident that would be even remarkable in everyday life. I have shorn my fiction of romance.

Charlotte Brontë, whose later work as a novelist shows the creative power of unexorcized longings, turned away from the engrossing fantasy of Angria towards the light of common day, bidding farewell in a passage in her journal which brings home the hospitable obsessional world of individual fantasy. She describes her vision of the aristocratic figures who peopled Angria:

> As I saw them stately and handsome, gliding through these saloons where many other well-known forms crossed my sight, where there were faces looking up, eyes smiling, and lips moving in audible speech that I knew better almost than my brothers and sisters, yet whose voices had never woke an echo in this world, whose eyes had never gazed upon that daylight, what glorious associations crowded upon me, . . . I know this house, I know the square it stands in. . . .

But in her diary she writes: 'Still, I long to quit for a while that burning clime where we have sojourned too long – its skies flame – the glow of sunset is always upon it – the mind would cease from excitement and turn now to a cooler region where the dawn breaks grey and sober, and the coming day for a time at least is subdued by clouds.'

The floridness of 'romance' offended against mid-Victorian realism in two principal ways. At first, because it was not concerned with the actual: social conditions, ordinary people, the common chances of life. Then, when emphasis upon the condition-of-England gave way in the late eighteen-fifties to a preoccupation with psychological realism, it offended because of its tendency to simplify and allegorize character, to offer tableaux instead of the processes of choosing. Many of the novels called 'romances' by mid-Victorian critics were indeed trivial. But one figure, whose immense influence on Victorian and Edwardian fiction has not yet been fully understood, stands out. Hawthorne adopted the romance as a form of fiction for exploring other territories than those explored in the novel. *The Scarlet Letter* was first published in England in 1850. In *The American Novel and Its Tradition* (London, 1958) Richard Chase points out that 'the element of romance has been far more noticeable in the American novel than in the English', and that American writers such as Hawthorne,

Melville and Poe 'have found uses for romance far beyond the escapism, fantasy, and sentimentality often associated with it'.

Hawthorne's novels, *The Scarlet Letter*, *The House of the Seven Gables*, *The Marble Faun*, and his tales such as 'The Gentle Boy' and 'Dr Heidegger's Experiment' suggest elements of the historical novel, the Gothic novel, the supernatural and the allegorical. He uses all these elements with an excruciating gentleness of touch to penetrate the psychological fastnesses of his characters' beings and to suggest the psychic states of the societies they inhabit. *The Scarlet Letter* resolves into a succession of mythic tableaux, outside the prison, in the forest, on the scaffold. He uses 'the attempt to connect a bygone time with the very present that is flitting away from us' as a means to forge a link between myth and history, and between the life of the individual and the covert processes of the society he inhabits.

In the Preface to *The House of the Seven Gables* (1851) subtitled *A Romance*, he sets out the distinction between romance and novel.

When a writer calls his work a Romance, it need hardly be observed that he wishes to claim a certain latitude, both as to its fashion and material, which he would not have felt himself entitled to assume had he professed to be writing a Novel. The latter form of composition is presumed to aim at a very minute fidelity, not merely to the possible, but to the probable and ordinary course of man's experience. The former – while, as a work of art, it must rigidly subject itself to laws, and while it sins unpardonably so far as it may swerve aside from the truth of the human heart – has fairly a right to present that truth under circumstances, to a great extent, of the writer's own choosing or creation. If he think fit, also, he may so manage his atmospherical medium as to bring out or mellow the lights and deepen and enrich the shadows of the picture. He will be wise, no doubt, to make a very moderate use of the privileges here stated, and, especially, to mingle the Marvellous rather as a slight, delicate, and evanescent flavor, than any portion of the actual substance of the dish offered to the public.

In his imagery of light – an imagery which pervades his work –

the key words here are 'mellow', 'deepen' and 'enrich'. For Hawthorne, the romance explores the fertile darkness beneath the surface of personality. It affords intimacy with what is obscure within us. We see here, stirring, an idea which has obsessed artists in our own century: the last undiscovered country this side of the grave is the territory of the unconscious mind.

The faintly defensive, humorous tone of Hawthorne's Preface probably reflects the low intellectual status associated with 'the romance' when set in contradistinction to the novel. But other Victorian novelists were attracted by its empirical freedom, its un-analytical symbolism, as George Eliot's 'The Lifted Veil' and *Silas Marner* show. The idea of the romance as a possible alternative mode of fiction gathered strength in the eighteen-seventies. George Meredith, the most influential novelist consciously to weigh it against realistic methods in his fiction, always distrusted the sim-plified motives and character-presentation of romance, however:

> Your fair one of Romance cannot suffer a mishap without a plotting villain, perchance many of them, to wreak the dread iniquity: she cannot move without him; she is the marble block, and if she is to have a feature, he is the sculptor; she depends on him for life, and her human history at least is married to him far more than to the rescuing lover.
>
> *(Diana of the Crossways*, Ch. XXXV (1885))

Earlier in his career in 1871 he had written the novel which was to be adopted by Robert Louis Stevenson and other younger writers as an example of the rich artistic potentialities of romance's liberated experience. *The Adventures of Harry Richmond* sets ideal worlds against the demands of the actual. Harry's father is a royal pretender; the woman he loves is the Princess of a seemingly fairy-tale German state. The book is a *Bildungsroman*: it shows the hero's growth towards self-consciousness and maturity. He develops through the marvels of childhood, the extremities of adolescence, to a stable, even ordinary adult self. He is obliged gradually to renounce his father's grandiose, imaginative life – the simplified world of the omnipotent ego. Meredith recognizes that romance draws upon primary sources of experience, that we have all in our time been princes and giants and royal pretenders. He gives this fantasy world an unstable yet robust presence in actuality through the figure of Richmond Roy. The book's argument places and scales down the 'fabulous' and the 'marvellous'; but much of its energy comes from the irresponsible power generated by Richmond Roy.

In one dazzling scene Meredith creates a moment which dramatizes the problematical relationship between the romance and the novel. Harry Richmond rediscovers his lost father, encased in metal, impersonating a bronze statue of a prince on horseback. The meeting is absurd and poignant. The human figure of the pretender struggles to be free of his trappings in order to embrace his son:

> The head of the statue turned from Temple to me.
> I found the people falling back with amazed exclamations. I – so prepossessed was I – simply stared at the sudden-flashing white of the statue's eyes. The eyes, from being an instant ago dull carved balls, were animated. they were fixed on me. I was unable to give out a breath. Its chest heaved; both bronze hands struck against the bosom.
> 'Richmond! my son! Richie! Harry Richmond! Richmond Roy!'
> That was what the statue gave forth.
> My head was like a ringing pan. I knew it was my father, but my father with death and strangeness, earth, metal, about him; and his voice was like a human cry contending with earth and metal – mine was stifled. I saw him descend. I dismounted. We met at the ropes and embraced. All his figure was stiff, smooth, cold. My arms slid on him. Each time he spoke I thought it an unnatural thing: I myself had not spoken once. (Ch. XVI)

The symbolic suggestions of the meeting comment not only on the relationship of father and son but upon the forms of experience they represent: the hieratic, stiffened, yet ebullient energy of the father's search for kingship; the son's humble difficult attempt to sustain relationships and emotions, which the wonder of his childhood circumstances have almost stunned in him. The novel is subtly balanced between the claims of myth and analysis, the ego and society. It is not simply a free-wheeling 'romance': what it does have is the quality Henry James described as the one characteristic generally ascribable to romance: 'experience liberated'.

'Experience liberated': the need for liberation was felt especially strongly by writers in the eighteen-eighties, since fiction was at the time largely dominated by the determinism of the French Naturalist novelists. The movement towards 'romance', which has been well illustrated in Kenneth Graham's *English Criticism of the Novel 1865–1900* (Oxford, 1965), was in part escapism, certainly: a determination to enjoy again objects *couleur de rose* in reaction to the emphasis on the inescapable animality of man's fate, demonstrated in Zola, Huysmans, and the brothers Goncourt. But it was also an assertion of free-will, of free experience as an expression of choice and personality.

It is easy to overestimate the extent to which even the French Naturalists insisted upon the purely animal. Huysmans's *En Rade* uses dream sequences, and Zola, who believed in separating dreams and actuality, devoted one of his Rougon-Macquart novels, *Le Rêve*, to dream. But these dreams share the brutality of waking life. In *Germinal* the climactic sequence of the book has many of the characteristics we have earlier associated with the romance. The two rivals, Chaval and Étienne, and Cathérine, the girl they love, are trapped alone together in the mine; Étienne kills Chaval and at last wins Cathérine. Here we have a love-story, combat, withdrawal from society, private ideals, emotional extremity, the ecstatic fulfilment of long-suppressed wishes – but these elements are held within a larger symbol of what society has done to these individuals and to all the dead miners who lie around them. They are trapped and brutalized, starved and fever-ridden, though for a

F

brief moment of peace the lovers reach bliss. A momentary pastoral creates itself for Cathérine: the ringing of her ears sounds like bird-song and the great yellow patches swimming in front of her eyes are so large that she thinks she is out of doors, near the canal, in the meadows on a fine summer day. But we can never forget the stench, the starvation, the approach of death. The enclosed Bower of Bliss, the Pleasure Dome, has changed terribly into the black imprisonment of the Voreux mine. In the eighteenth century the opposition between 'romance' and 'reality' was seen in terms of a contrast between the 'marvellous 'and rationalism; now the conflict was rather between the *individualism* of romance and the inexorable processes of society.

THE RECONCILIATION OF 'ROMANCE' AND 'REALISM'

The critical argument between the claims of 'realism' and 'romance' in the later nineteenth century exaggerated the contrast between the two modes and its attempt to establish them as separate categories was bound to fail for all but a very few works. Dickens in the first number of *Household Words* (1849) spoke of the service-ability of light literature:

> To show all, that in all familiar things, even in those which are repellent on the surface, there is Romance enough, if we will find it out – to teach the hardest workers at this whirling wheel of toil that their lot is not necessarily a moody brutal fact excluded from the sympathies and graces of imagination.

Revealing the 'Romance' in common life became a preoccupation for the generation of English writers who followed the French Naturalists and were influenced by them. Arnold Bennett and H. G. Wells both sought to combine the humdrum and the imaginative in such a way that the inner qualities of the individual's experience would be realized without a corresponding idealization of the social setting. In Bennett's *Hilda Lessways*, for example, the

narrator, appropriating and expanding the character's consciousness, comments at the beginning of an interview between Hilda and
George

> She saw glimpses, beautiful and compensatory, of the romantic
> quality of common life. She was in a little office of a perfectly ordinary
> boarding-house – (she could even detect stale odours of cooking) –
> with a realistic man of business, and they were about to discuss a
> perfectly ordinary piece of scandal; and surely they might be called
> two common-sense people! And withal, the ordinariness and the
> midland gumption of the scene were shot through with the bright
> exotic rays of romance!
>
> (Ch. 2, section 3)

In his social novels H. G. Wells deliberately invokes echoes of
older romance worlds to suggest the imagination's power to
transform its surroundings: we have 'the Romance of Commerce'
in *Tono-Bungay*. In *The History of Mr Polly* the scene of Mr
Polly's adoring courtship of the upper-class schoolgirl (she
sitting on the park wall above him, he pleading from below,
beside his bicycle) is cast in the language of knight-errantry. The
effect is not entirely comic, or even mock-heroic. The language
suggests the emotional lyricism of Mr Polly's experience, even
while its stilted images remind us of the phantasmal quality of this
love affair. In the last section of the book Mr Polly takes on the role
of knight-errant in a more meaningful way: he saves the Plump
Woman, her niece and the Potwell Inn from the depredations of the
criminal, Jim, in a series of personal battles which are exhilarating,
comic and heroic. His reward is a return to the pastoral. The
imagery of romance was still alive for Wells as an expression of the
imaginative aspirations which modern lower-class education and
conditions too often tragically stunted: their lives, cut off from
literature, are, he writes in *Kipps*, divorced 'from the apprehension
of beauty that we favoured ones are given – the vision of the
Grail that makes life fine for ever.'

Romance has become a quality, an imaginative power immanent in the 'real' world for those who are able to apprehend it. Conrad; who always resisted critical attempts to classify his work as either 'romantic or realistic', insisting that it was 'purely temperamental', wrote in the preface to *The Shadow Line*:

> The world of the living contains enough marvels and mysteries as it is; marvels and mysteries acting upon our emotions and intelligence in ways so inexplicable that it would almost justify the conception of life as an enchanted state.

The Shadow Line, with its echoes of *The Ancient Mariner*, its extraordinary imaginative authority which invokes the supernatural and the allegorical without ever relinquishing natural causes, transforms romance into morality. Conrad himself saw it as an expression of identity with the suffering of the First World War generation.

In the twentieth century the conflict between 'romance' and 'realism' has lessened because writers have emphasized the extent to which each man carries within him an obscure and separate universe. The subjectivism of romance has become the common artistic attitude. The remote, the exotic, are harboured in each man: relativism triumphs. Yet at the same time Freud and Jung have reminded artists of the extent to which all impulses and emblems are common property. In *Ulysses* we see an achieved and conscious fusion of psychological realism with the romance form. In the nineteenth century, works which continued to be called 'romances' rarely used the traditional narrative techniques of prose romance – the apparent prolixity, the easy way of calling back into activity episodes and characters long abandoned, the burgeoning of story out of story. When this narrative rhythm is lost some of the peculiar qualities of romance experience vanish: the infinitely supple tension, the prolific and apparently disorderly inclusiveness, the way in which events engender a whole range of disconnected happenings whose connections are yet felt though never pointed, the onward drift which dissolves the present into the past and remakes new presents which themselves dislimn. These narrative methods make the experience of reading the romances close to the experiencing of life.

The great nineteenth-century novelists of social life, Balzac and Dickens, adopted something of the same fecund inclusive narrative growth. Joyce, in *Ulysses*, adopts the romance organization as a consciously controlled method of presenting life's ample contingencies. Bloom, the wandering Jew or errant knight, or epic Ulysses, travels through Dublin which is his home yet alien to him. He experiences without amazement, though with zest, all the particularity which his senses offer him, while at the same time, dream, illusion, wishes and memory create the inner present. Joyce frequently refers to the old Irish romances and sometimes the language converts Bloom momentarily into a traditional, and absurd, heroic figure:

> Who comes through Michan's land, bedight in sable armour? O'Bloom, the son of Rory: it is he. Impervious to fear is Rory's son: he of the prudent soul.

The free flow of consciousness in *Ulysses*, the authoritarian mastery of Joyce, the way in which incidents and significances cut across each other, the variety of style, the robust tranquillity (which some mistake for coldness), all turn the novel full circle to embrace – and overwhelm – the romance.

5
Conclusion

The romance has always flourished in periods of rapid change: twelfth-century France, Elizabethan England, the end of the eighteenth century. We might expect to find it flourishing in our own time. Although what Yeats called 'the gentleness of old romance' has changed into the insipidity of women's magazine fiction, other romance elements survive in new guises. The 'ideal worlds' of works such as Mervyn Peake's *Gormenghast* trilogy and Tolkien's *Lord of the Rings* cycle emphasize the grotesque and the menacing. They both offer totally imagined idiosyncratic worlds which we can inhabit completely while we read; and both worlds are preoccupied with complex moral issues, acted out by characters living according to a conscious code of conduct. They instruct us in our own world even while they allow us to escape from it. They express the conserving and crystallizing function of romance.

In science fiction we find a mode which questions in an often revolutionary way, our assumptions about our own world. (H. G. Wells called his early works, such as *The War of the Worlds*, 'scientific romances'.) Such stories are wilful fictions, in which we have to depend almost entirely upon the writer's authority; provided that he offers us a congruent vision and persuades us to accept his 'impossibilities' he is at liberty to shape experience as he likes. This is the point of descent from the romance. Throughout its history romance has relied upon direct sense impressions to bring close its imagined worlds. Science fiction plays upon this by distorting our sense expectations and making us think through again the material means by which we reach judgements. Its 'ideal' worlds are more often nightmares than serene gardens. The element of sense-dislocation emphasizes the grotesque. It releases us from the ordinary conditions of life. But it obliges us to look back at life, and our assumptions about the possibilities of life, with cold re-appraisal.

Romance, being absorbed with the ideal, always has an element of prophecy. It remakes the world in the image of desire. At present, however, such prophetic literature tends to resolve into images of dread. The function of romance in our own time may well prove to have been not wish-fulfilment but exorcism.

Select Bibliography

Anyone wanting to study the development of the romance could well begin by reading the works discussed or mentioned in the text of this study. They are all listed in the index. In addition, GEOFFREY OF MONMOUTH'S *Historia regum Britanniae* is available in translation in Penguin Classics as is GOTTFRIED VON STRASSBURG'S *Tristan*, and the *Mabinogion*.

The romance is still fertile in children's literature. For fine examples see works by Alan Garner and Edward Ardizzone. I have listed below critical works which are valuable for an understanding of the romance. By no means all of them are exclusively concerned with this subject.

General

ALLOTT, M., *Novelists on the Novel*, London, 1959.

See especially chapter I 'The Novel and the Marvellous'.

AUERBACH, E., *Mimesis*, Princeton, 1953.

An overarching account of the types of 'reality' in literature. It includes a penetrating analysis of Chrétien de Troyes.

BEATTIE, J., 'On Fable and Romance', *Dissertations Moral and Critical*, 2 vols, Dublin, 1783.

An early historical essay on the genre.

D'ARCY, M. C., *The Mind and Heart of Love. Lion and Unicorn: A Study in Eros and Agape*, London, 1945.

FRYE, N., *The Anatomy of Criticism*, Princeton, 1957.

A vital modern interpretation of the function of myth in literature. See particularly the third and fourth essays.

KERMODE, F., *The Sense of an Ending*, New York, 1967.
A brilliant analysis of the forms of fiction and particularly of its 'prophetic' function.

HOGGART, R., *The Uses of Literacy*, London, 1957.

LUKÁCS, G., *The Historical Novel*, tr. H. & S. Mitchell, London, 1962.
An influential Marxist interpretation of the relationship between fiction and society. See particularly the discussion of 'type' characters.

REEVE, C., *The Progress of Romance*, London, 1785.
Still one of the most stimulating accounts of the romance form. Penetrating and amusing.

ROUGEMONT, D. DE, *Passion and Society*, tr. M. Belgion, rev. ed., London, 1956.
An attempt to characterize love and its literary meaning in Western society.

SAINTSBURY, G., *The Flourishing of Romance*, Edinburgh, 1899.

SCOTT, W., *On Romance*, Edinburgh, 1824.

WATT, I., *The Rise of the Novel*, London, 1957.
On 'formal realism' in the novel, which he sees as displacing the romance.

WELLEK, R. and WARREN, A., *The Theory of Literature*, New York, 1949.

Medieval to Renaissance Romance

ARTHOS, J., *On the Poetry of Spenser and the Form of Romances*, London, 1956.

BARBER, R. W., *Arthur of Albion: an Introduction to the Arthurian Literature and Legends of England*, London, 1961.

CRANE, R. S., *The Vogue of Medieval Chivalric Romance during the English Renaissance*, Menasha, 1919.

DANBY, J., *Poets on Fortune's Hill*, London, 1952.

Especially the chapters on 'The Great House Romance' and Arcadia and Shakespeare's last plays.

EVERETT, D., 'A Characterization of the English Medieval Romances', *Essays and Studies*, XV, 1929.

FINLAYSON, J., ed., *Morte Arthure*, London, 1967.

Distinguishes helpfully between romance and *chanson de geste*.

FRAPPIER, J., *Chrétien de Troyes*, Paris, 1957.

An outstanding critical study.

GRIFFIN, N. E., 'The Definition of Romance', *P.M.L.A.*, XXXVIII, 1923.

Distinguishes between 'epic' and 'romance' with epic as indigenous, romance as exotic material.

HALL, V., *Renaissance Literary Criticisms*, New York, 1945.

HEER, F., *The Medieval World*, tr. J. Sondheimer, London, 1962.

Especially Chapter 7, 'Courtly Love and Courtly Literature'.

HOUGH, G., *A Preface to The Faerie Queene*, London, 1962.

HUNTER, G. K., *John Lyly*, London, 1962.

LEWIS, C. S., *The Allegory of Love*, London, 1936.

LOOMIS, R. S., *The Development of Arthurian Romance*, London, 1963.

PETTET, E. C., *Shakespeare and the Romance Tradition*, London, 1949.

RENWICK, W. L. and ORTON, H., *The Beginnings of English Literature*, 3rd. ed. rev., London, 1966.

Especially the section on Romances. A valuable critical bibliography.

SPEIRS, J., *Medieval English Poetry: The Non-Chaucerian Tradition*, London, 1957. Parts III and IV.

TUVE, R., *Allegorical Imagery: Some Medieval Books and their Posterity*, Princeton, 1966.

Especially chapter 5, 'Romances'. A deeply penetrating examination of the relationships between Spenser and the romances.

VINAVER, E., ed., *The Works of Sir Thomas Malory*, 3 vols, Oxford, 1947.

VINAVER, E., *Form and Meaning in Medieval Romance*, Modern Humanities Research Association, 1966.

A brief masterly essay.

WESTON, J., *From Ritual to Romance*, Cambridge, 1920.

Best-known for its bearing on Eliot's *The Waste Land*, which could well be studied in the context of a history of the romance form.

Post-Renaissance Romance

CHASE, R., *The American Novel and Its Tradition*, London, 1958.

CONRAD, J., Preface to *The Shadow Line*.

GRAHAM, K., *English Criticism of the Novel 1865–1900*, Oxford, 1965.

Especially vii, 'The Rise of the Romance'.

HUET, D., *Traite de l'Origine des Romans*, Paris, 1670.

HURD, R., *Letters on Chivalry and Romance*, London, 1762.

First sustained defence of romances against mid-eighteenth century attacks.

JAMES, H., Preface to *The American*, first printed in the New York edition of the *Novels and Stories* (1907–17), Vol II.

JOHNSON, S., *Rambler*, no. 4, 1750.

This essay is a *locus classicus* for the distinction between novel and romance.

LANG, A., 'Realism and Romance', *Contemporary Review*, LIII, 1887.

Part of an extended debate carried on in this journal at the time.

MATTHEWS, J. H., *Surrealism and the Novel*, Ann Arbor, 1966.

A suggestive analysis of the romance elements revived in surrealist fiction.

MEHROTRA, K. K., *Horace Walpole and the English Novel*, Oxford, 1934.
Carefully documented history of the rise of the Gothic novel.
RILEY, E. C., *Cervantes's Theory of the Novel*, Oxford, 1962.
STEVENSON, R. L., 'A Humble Remonstrance', *Longmans' Magazine*, V, 1884.
Defence of 'the romance' against the demands of realism.
VARMA, DEVENDRA, *The Gothic Flame*, London, 1957.

Volume 2 of the present series (LILIAN FURST, *Romanticism*) gives a helpful bibliography, some of which will be found relevant to the study of the romance in the late eighteenth and early nineteenth centuries.

Index